Android Application Development with Maven

Learn how to use and configure Maven to support all phases of the development of an Android application

Patroklos Papapetrou

Jonathan LALOU

BIRMINGHAM - MUMBAI

Android Application Development with Maven

First published: March 2015

Production reference: 1160315

Published by Packt Publishing Ltd.
Livery Place
35 Livery Street
Birmingham B3 2PB, UK.

ISBN 978-1-78398-610-1

www.packtpub.com

Credits

Authors
Patroklos Papapetrou

Jonathan LALOU

Reviewers
Daniel Beland

David Bernard

Brad Leege

Sujit Pal

Commissioning Editor
Akram Hussain

Acquisition Editor
Harsha Bharwani

Content Development Editor
Mohammed Fahad

Technical Editor
Abhishek R. Kotian

Copy Editors
Nithya P

Adithi Shetty

Project Coordinator
Danuta Jones

Proofreaders
Maria Gould

Lesley Harrison

Clyde Jenkins

Indexer
Mariammal Chettiyar

Graphics
Abhinash Sahu

Production Coordinator
Aparna Bhagat

Cover Work
Aparna Bhagat

About the Authors

Patroklos Papapetrou is a software architect addicted to software quality and an agile team leader with more than 15 years of experience in software engineering. His expertise lies in Android and Java development. He believes and invests in people and team spirit, seeking quality excellence. He's one of the authors of the book *SonarQube in Action*, *Manning Publications* and his next writing attempt will be *The Art of Software Gardening*. He treats software systems like flowers; that's why he prefers to call himself a software gardener.

He's also an occasional speaker, conducting talks about clean code, Android development, code quality, and software gardening.

I'd like to thank my loving and beautiful wife, Anna, for her patience all these months, especially during the weekends. Without her encouragement, I wouldn't have managed to finish my part of the book. Thanks to my sons, Panagiotis (age 6) and Charis (4-years old), who understood that sometimes, daddy couldn't play with them or go to the park. You can have me back now! Thanks to our families for their patience as well and for sometimes watching the kids to let me work on the book.

Jonathan LALOU is an engineer fascinated by new technologies, computer sciences, and the digital world since his childhood. A graduate of the Ecole des Mines — one of the best French polytechnic institutes — Jonathan has more than 14 years of experience in Java and the JEE ecosystem.

Jonathan has worked for several global companies and financial institutions, such as Syred, Philips, Sungard, Ixis CIB, BNP Paribas, and Amundi AM. He has strong ties, daily contacts, and frequent trips in Western Europe, Northern America, Judea, and emerging Asia. During his career, Jonathan has successfully climbed many levels: developer, architect, Scrum master, team leader, and project manager.

Now, Jonathan is CTO at SayaSoft (`http://www.sayasoft.fr`), a digital company focused on very high value added projects he founded with two partners. SayaSoft brings Java environment, migration of small and large organizations to agility, and Android development to a new level. SayaSoft's customers are ensured to get high-quality releases and quick ROI.

Jonathan's skills include a wide range of technologies and frameworks, such as Spring, JPA/Hibernate, GWT, Mule ESB, JSF/PrimeFaces, Groovy, Android, EJB, JMS, application servers, agile methods, and, of course, Apache Maven.

Jonathan also authored *Apache Maven Dependency Management*, published by Packt Publishing in October 2013.

Jonathan is available on the cloud. You can read his blog at `http://jonathan.lalou.free.fr`, catch him on Twitter at `http://twitter.com/john_the_cowboy`, and find him on LinkedIn at `http://www.linkedin.com/in/jonathanlalou`.

About the Reviewers

Daniel Beland was an early adopter of Maven 1.0 from 2004 and has since used it in many projects across diverse industries, ranging from Formula One, Music, DNA laboratories to Defense and Security.

He currently works for Thales' Research and Technology Center in Quebec City, Canada, where part of his work has been to develop cognitive assessment tools for Android devices.

David Bernard is an experienced software developer. Over the past 15 years, he worked as a freelancer for the bank, automotive, and game industries.

He also contributed to a lot of open source projects. He is the creator of several plugins for Maven, Gradle, jEdit, Netbeans, Eclipse, Blender, and so on. His current interest is in 3D and the gamedev pipeline.

He shares his latest contributions on GitHub at `http://github.com/davidB`.

Brad Leege has a myriad of software development experience from across a variety of industries as well as the public sector. This has given him the passion for open source and open data and the desire to share it with others.

Sujit Pal is a Java/Python programmer, whose main areas of interest are information retrieval, distributed processing, natural language processing, and machine learning. He was an early adopter and proponent of Maven at his company. He loves what he does for a living, believes in lifelong learning, and shares his experiences at `http://sujitpal.blogspot.in/`.

He works for Healthline Networks, Inc., a startup in the consumer healthcare space.

It has been a pleasure to review this book. Special thanks to the author and the publishing team for making the process so enjoyable.

www.PacktPub.com

Support files, eBooks, discount offers, and more

For support files and downloads related to your book, please visit www.PacktPub.com.

Did you know that Packt offers eBook versions of every book published, with PDF and ePub files available? You can upgrade to the eBook version at www.PacktPub.com and as a print book customer, you are entitled to a discount on the eBook copy. Get in touch with us at service@packtpub.com for more details.

At www.PacktPub.com, you can also read a collection of free technical articles, sign up for a range of free newsletters and receive exclusive discounts and offers on Packt books and eBooks.

https://www2.packtpub.com/books/subscription/packtlib

Do you need instant solutions to your IT questions? PacktLib is Packt's online digital book library. Here, you can search, access, and read Packt's entire library of books.

Why subscribe?

- Fully searchable across every book published by Packt
- Copy and paste, print, and bookmark content
- On demand and accessible via a web browser

Free access for Packt account holders

If you have an account with Packt at www.PacktPub.com, you can use this to access PacktLib today and view 9 entirely free books. Simply use your login credentials for immediate access.

Table of Contents

Preface

During the months we were writing this book, a lot of people asked us what would make this book special and why someone should care to read it. The most powerful argument that I heard all this time was, "Hey, Google official supports only Gradle to build Android applications and the latest release of Android Studio makes extensive use of Gradle. Ant was already replaced and Maven is nowhere. Why do you spend time writing about developing Android applications with Maven?"

Good questions! The answers, however, is hidden within the question itself. First of all, there are no books out there that explain step by step about all the development phases and critical tasks to build and manage the life cycle of an Android Application with Maven. Maven is still—no matter if we like it or not—the most popular build tool. Many "traditional" software houses that have invested time and efforts to standardize their development process around Maven want to make the next step and expand their portfolio to the Android Market. Clearly, having another build tool only for Android development doesn't look very practical, although it's an option.

Companies would save a lot of money if they could just plug their Android applications to the existing development life cycle, driven by Maven. At the same time, it's true that Maven is a very mature, flexible, and robust build tool. Its extensibility through plugins and the idea of descriptively configuring the build process without the need to write scripts made it the de-facto standard.

The reality, however, has shown us that it's not always that easy. Maven provides all the required plugins to do almost everything, but there are no instructions or well-structured documentation. You can find blog posts here and there that shortly cover some topics but this is not enough.

This book aims to fill that gap. It will not teach you how to write Android applications, although you will find some simple examples. It will guide you, however, from A to Z, about how to set up all the necessary Maven configuration to compile, run, test, deploy, release, and verify the quality of an Android application. It's convenient for both experienced and young Android developers because we provide all the example code to see Maven in action. This book is also for those of you who already have some Maven experience but feel lost when you try to integrate it with your Android development process.

You can read the book sequentially if you have little experience with Maven, but you can also use it as a reference and jump to any chapter you want as each one is dedicated to a particular topic. The provided code is separated in different folders per chapter so that you can easily run the examples and verify that you have correctly followed the instructions of the book.

We are confident that you will find the book useful and practical, and we hope that it will help you build your next Android application with Maven.

What this book covers

Chapter 1, Beginning with the Basics, introduces you to the basic concepts of Maven and guides you to install all the required software you need to develop an Android application with Maven.

Chapter 2, Starting the Development Phase, sets the pace for the rest of the book. It discusses the first step to set up a minimal Maven configuration to compile and deploy an Android application to a real device or emulator.

Chapter 3, Unit Testing, covers several ways to write and run unit tests using various tools. It also explains the differences between unit and integration testing and the important role that both of them playing when developing an Android application.

Chapter 4, Integration Testing, completes the discussion about testing and presents three alternatives of running Android instrumentation tests, and also provides guidance on properly configuring Maven.

Chapter 5, Android Flavors, discusses the hot topic of maintaining multiple versions (free, ads-supported, and paid) of the same application. It describes the problem and then presents two ways to handle the case using Maven.

Chapter 6, Release Life Cycle and Continuous Integration, is all about releasing and deploying an Android application to a Maven repository. A bonus topic in this chapter discusses about automating everything using Jenkins, the most popular continuous integration engine.

Chapter 7, Other Tools and Plugins, is the last chapter and covers two very important topics: code quality with SonarQube and speeding up the development life cycle using the non-standard emulators provided by Android.

What you need for this book

This book is about software development, so you will need to install some tools in order to follow the examples and practices discussed. You can use almost all operating systems (Windows, Linux, and Mac OS) to run the code included in this book as most of the commands you will see run in a terminal window. All the other software required is covered mostly in *Chapter 1, Beginning with the Basics*, where we set up our development environment (SDKs, IDEs, and so on) so you don't need to pre-install anything. This also applies to the rest of the chapters when we demonstrate the integration of Maven with other popular tools. In general, don't worry if you don't have anything installed yet. We will guide you step by step. On the other hand, if you find yourself reading instructions about installing software you already have in your environment, feel free to skip it.

Who this book is for

Android Application Development with Maven is intended for Android developers or devops engineers who want to use Maven to effectively develop quality Android applications. Whether you are already using Maven or another build tool, this book focuses only on Maven topics that are related to the Android development. It would be helpful, but not necessary, if you have some previous experience with Maven.

Conventions

In this book, you will find a number of text styles that distinguish between different kinds of information. Here are some examples of these styles and an explanation of their meaning.

Code words in text, database table names, folder names, filenames, file extensions, pathnames, dummy URLs, user input, and Twitter handles are shown as follows: "A folder `target` containing a `chapter1.apk` archive should be created."

A block of code is set as follows:

```java
public class BookServiceImpl implements BookService {
  @Override
  public Book createBook(String title, String format, String
  color, Integer numberOfPages) {
    final Book book = new Book();
    book.setTitle(title);
    book.setFormat(format);
    book.setColor(color);
    book.setNumberOfPages(numberOfPages);
    return book;
  }
}
```

When we wish to draw your attention to a particular part of a code block, the relevant lines or items are set in bold:

```xml
<dependency>
  <groupId>${project.groupId}</groupId>
  <artifactId>contract</artifactId>
  <version>1.0-SNAPSHOT</version>
  <type>pom</type>
</dependency>
```

Any command-line input or output is written as follows:

```
$ANDROID_HOME//tools/android move avd --name Nexus_7_2012 --rename
Nexus_7_2012_bis
```

New terms and **important words** are shown in bold. Words that you see on the screen, for example, in menus or dialog boxes, appear in the text like this: "Clicking the **Next** button moves you to the next screen."

 Warnings or important notes appear in a box like this.

 Tips and tricks appear like this.

Reader feedback

Feedback from our readers is always welcome. Let us know what you think about this book—what you liked or disliked. Reader feedback is important for us as it helps us develop titles that you will really get the most out of.

To send us general feedback, simply e-mail feedback@packtpub.com, and mention the book's title in the subject of your message.

If there is a topic that you have expertise in and you are interested in either writing or contributing to a book, see our author guide at www.packtpub.com/authors.

Customer support

Now that you are the proud owner of a Packt book, we have a number of things to help you to get the most from your purchase.

Downloading the example code

You can download the example code files from your account at http://www.packtpub.com for all the Packt Publishing books you have purchased. If you purchased this book elsewhere, you can visit http://www.packtpub.com/support and register to have the files e-mailed directly to you.

Errata

Although we have taken every care to ensure the accuracy of our content, mistakes do happen. If you find a mistake in one of our books—maybe a mistake in the text or the code—we would be grateful if you could report this to us. By doing so, you can save other readers from frustration and help us improve subsequent versions of this book. If you find any errata, please report them by visiting http://www.packtpub.com/submit-errata, selecting your book, clicking on the **Errata Submission Form** link, and entering the details of your errata. Once your errata are verified, your submission will be accepted and the errata will be uploaded to our website or added to any list of existing errata under the Errata section of that title.

To view the previously submitted errata, go to https://www.packtpub.com/books/content/support and enter the name of the book in the search field. The required information will appear under the **Errata** section.

Piracy

Piracy of copyrighted material on the Internet is an ongoing problem across all media. At Packt, we take the protection of our copyright and licenses very seriously. If you come across any illegal copies of our works in any form on the Internet, please provide us with the location address or website name immediately so that we can pursue a remedy.

Please contact us at copyright@packtpub.com with a link to the suspected pirated material.

We appreciate your help in protecting our authors and our ability to bring you valuable content.

Questions

If you have a problem with any aspect of this book, you can contact us at questions@packtpub.com, and we will do our best to address the problem.

1
Beginning with the Basics

In this chapter, we will see how to download, install, and set up a development environment, including the essential elements: **Java Development Kit (JDK)**, **Apache Maven**, **Android SDK**, and an **Integrated Development Environment (IDE)**. There will be pictures and illustrations provided to help you progress as quickly as possible.

Throughout this work, we will assume that you have a basic knowledge of Java, system, Maven, and IDEs and are familiar with terms such as: compiler, environment variables, repository, plugin, goal, build, and so on.

Installing Java

Prior to anything else, download and install a JDK7 and optionally a **Java Runtime Environment (JRE)**. Both of them are downloadable from the Oracle website: `http://www.oracle.com/technetwork/java/javase/downloads/jdk7-downloads-1880260.html`. As a reminder, the JDK is a collection of tools needed to develop, compile, and monitor a Java application in the development state, whereas a JRE is needed to run a Java-compiled class or an archive. Keep in mind also that at the time this book was written, Android was not officially supporting JDK8 and that Oracle had already announced the end of public releases of JDK7. We hope that now that you read these lines, Android is compatible with the latest JDK. If not, then you should pick and install the latest available update of JDK7.

Set the environment variable `JAVA_HOME` to the right location, such as `/var/opt/java` or `C:\win32app\jdk_1.7.X` folder.

Then, add `$JAVA_HOME/bin` or `%JAVA_HOME%\bin` parameter to your `PATH` variable.

Check this by running the command `java -version` in a terminal. Here is an example of the expected output:

```
C:\>java -version
java version "1.7.0_45"
Java(TM) SE Runtime Environment (build 1.7.0_45-b18)
Java HotSpot(TM) Client VM (build 24.45-b08, mixed mode)
```

Download and Install Apache Maven

Download Maven 3.2.1 or greater from the Apache Maven website: `http://maven.apache.org/download.cgi`. Install this by uncompressing it in a folder of your choice. Set the environment variable `M2_HOME` to the right location, such as `/usr/lib/maven/` or `C:\win32app\apache-maven-3.2.1` folder.

Then, add `$M2_HOME/bin` or `%M2_HOME%\bin` parameter to your `PATH` variable. Check `mvn` setup is executable by running the command `mvn -version`. Here is an example of the expected output:

```
C:\win32app\Console-2.00.b148>mvn -version
Apache Maven 3.2.1 (ea8b2b07643dbb1b84b6d16e1f08391b666bc1e9; 2014-
02-14T18:37:52+01:00)
Maven home: C:\win32app\apache-maven-3.2.1
Java version: 1.7.0_45, vendor: Oracle CorporationJava home:
C:\win32app\jdk1.7.0_45\jre
Default locale: en_US, platform encoding: Cp1252
OS name: "windows 7", version: "6.1", arch: "x86", family: "windows"
```

Android SDK

Two ways exist to install the SDK: the former is faster but it hides several operations you should be aware of as an Android developer. The latter takes more time but it introduces you to the tools and concepts coming with the SDK. Besides, this allows you to customize your installation, such as the folders. If you are a beginner, we encourage you to follow the first approach. You can always tune Android SDK at a later time when you feel more confident and you are familiar with the available settings.

Android development tools

You can download and install the official Android Studio from the Android website: `https://developer.android.com/sdk/index.html`. Android Studio is a suite that includes an integrated development environment (Android IDE), based on **IntelliJ IDEA**, with Android SDK tools, as well as other stuff like an embedded emulator system image and platform tools.

For Windows users, after downloading the installer (`.exe` file), run it and just follow the instructions provided by the installer. You can keep the default values suggested if you are a beginner or if you are not sure how each setting affects the installation. When you're done, you can run Android Studio by clicking on the icon created by the installer.

For Linux users, unzip the file you downloaded to your favorite application directory. Then, navigate to the `android-studio/bin/` directory in a terminal and execute `studio.sh` command. Regardless of your operating system, always double-check before the installation that you have enough disk space. It varies from OS to OS.

Android SDK standalone

Alternately, if you already have an installed IDE or text editor, you can install the SDK manually. The following operations are long and tedious; however, any real Android developer should experience them at least once.

Download Android SDK from Android website: `https://developer.android.com/sdk/index.html#Other`. Again for Windows users, it is highly recommended to download the executable installer and follow the steps provided. Linux users can uncompress the downloaded zipped file to the folder of their choice, let's say `/home/dev/android-sdk` folder. In both cases, let's call the location where android SDK installed: `ANDROID_HOME` variable.

By default, the SDK has the following top-level directory tree:

Let's explore and review the content of the starter SDK:

- `%ANDROID_HOME%\tools\`: This folder gathers general utilities needed to develop, test, and debug an application.

- `%ANDROID_HOME%\platform-tools\`: This folder contains other utilities, such as `adb` and `fastboot`, needed by developers to design, code, and debug an application on an actual device.

- `%ANDROID_HOME%\add-ons\`: This folder is initially empty. It will be filled in later on, in order to provide support to call and use Google APIs, for instance the API allowing applications to communicate and display data from Google Maps.

- `%ANDROID_HOME%\AVD Manager.exe`: This parameter allows us to manage the **Android Virtual Devices (AVD)**, which are mere emulators. On first launch, no AVD is available. The following screenshot shows the **Android Virtual Device Manager**:

The AVD you will create later will be stored in your personal folder under the `.android/avd` path.

To launch the SDK manager, if you are a Windows user, run `%ANDROID_HOME%\SDK Manager.exe` command. If you are working on Linux, open a terminal and navigate to the tools/directory in the Android SDK and then execute:

`android sdk.`

In a first step like that shown in the following screenshot, install the packages suggested by the SDK Manager: SDK Tools, SDK Platform tools, the current API, and so on:

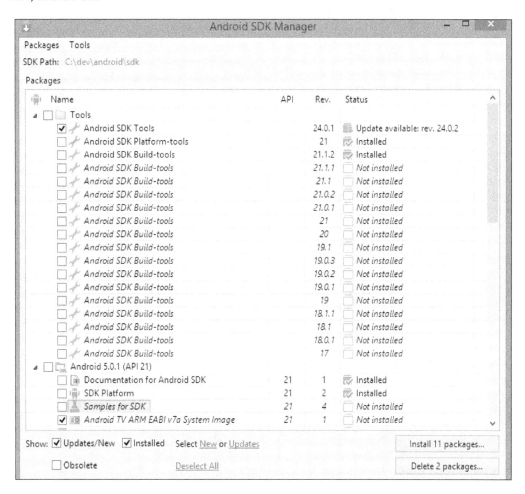

At the time of writing, the last version of Android is 5.0.1 **Lollipop**. The API level is different from the grand public version: Lollipop corresponds to API 21, as well as Android KitKat 4.4.2 did to API 19, Android 4.0 / IceCreamSandwich did to API 17, or Android 2.3.X / Gingerbread to API 10, and so on.

Accept the license agreements as shown in the next screenshot, and let SDK Manager download. This may take a while for the default set of packages , and will take longer if you add other packages to the install list.

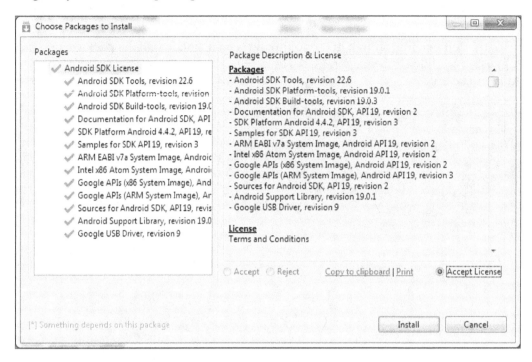

Once this is done, the directory tree will change a lot. The different folders are filled in with the elements selected in the preceding screenshot, such as Google APIs, drivers, documentation, sources, build tools, and so on.

Creation of a new project

Now, we create a new, basic project. Often, you may prefer to do this within your IDE; anyway, creating a project with Maven and its artifacts and then importing the new project into the IDE are more elegant practice: this will ensure the project matches Android standards and is not IDE-dependent. Moreover, by default, creating an Android project in an IDE and then adding Maven support to this require some tricks and hacks.

The first step needs a bit of work: determining the `platform.version` properties of your Android install. Go to one among the installed platforms folder. If you have downloaded only the latest SDK version, then it should be in the `ANDROID_HOME/platforms/android-21` folder. Open the file `source.properties`. Search for `Platform.Version` and `Pkg.Revision` properties. In the following sample file, the respective values are *4.4.2* and *3*:

```
AndroidVersion.ApiLevel=21
Layoutlib.Api=12
Layoutlib.Revision=2
Pkg.Desc=Android SDK Platform 5.0.1
Pkg.License=(…)
Pkg.LicenseRef=android-sdk-license
Pkg.Revision=2
Pkg.SourceUrl=https\://dl-ssl.google.com/android/repository/
repository-10.xml
Platform.MinToolsRev=22
Platform.Version=5.0.1
```

This allows us to conclude that the `Platform.Version` value is 5.0.1_r2. This is actually the combination of the properties: `Platform.Version` and `Pkg.Revision`. Note this value well as we will need to use it in a few places.

For the following Maven commands, you are assumed to have set the `ANDROID_HOME` environment variable; otherwise, you will need to suffix all the commands with the property `-Dandroid.sdk.path=/path/to/Android/SDK/install`. Now, we need to install the `android.jar` file as any regular Maven artifact in our local repository:

```
mvn install:install-file \

-Dfile=%ANDROID_HOME%\platforms\android-21\android.jar \

-DgroupId=com.google.android \

-DartifactId=android \

-Dversion=5.0.1_r2  \

-Dpackaging=jar \

-DgeneratePom=true
```

Unfortunately, you will have to perform this operation for each Android platform version your application will support. Yet, for Android artifacts prior to 4.1.1.4 (included), the corresponding archives are accessible via **Maven Central Repository**.

 In a later chapter, we will see how to automate the installation of Android artifacts in local repository.

Open a terminal, run the command as follows:

```
mvn archetype:generate \
  -DarchetypeArtifactId=android-quickstart \
  -DarchetypeGroupId=de.akquinet.android.archetypes \
  -DarchetypeVersion=1.1.0 \
  -DgroupId=com.packt.androidMaven \
  -DartifactId=chapter \
  -Dversion=1.0-SNAPSHOT \
  -Dplatform=21 \
  --batch-mode \
  --quiet
```

Then, a new folder `chapter1` is created. Go to this folder. You should find the tree of a classic Android project:

```
├───assets
├───res
│   ├───drawable-hdpi
│   ├───drawable-mdpi
│   ├───drawable-xhdpi
│   ├───drawable-xxhdpi
│   ├───layout
│   ├───menu
│   ├───values
│   ├───values-sw600dp
│   ├───values-sw720dp-land
│   ├───values-v11
│   └───values-v14
└───src
    └───main
        └───java
            └───com
                └───packt
                    └───androidMaven
```

At the root of the project is the **Project Object Model (POM)**, serialized as a pom.xml file. Beware that the pom.xml file is a representation of the actual POM, but discrepancies do exist between the actual POM and the pom.xml file.

Open the POM file in write mode with any regular text editor. Check the <platform.version> tag. This contains the same value as retrieved earlier (in our case: 5.0.1_r2); if it does not, then set it.

You can run a successful `mvn` setup clean installation. A folder `target` containing a `chapter1.apk` archive should be created. Theoretically, this **APK** file (short for, **Android PacKage**) can run on a compatible Android device, such as a smart phone, a tablet, or even a smart watch.

Debug Certificate expired

If you get a build failure with an error similar to the following:

```
[ERROR] Failed to execute goal
com.jayway.maven.plugins.android.generation2:android-
maven-plugin:3.8.2:apk (default-apk) on project
helloWorld: Debug Certificate expired on 02/02/13 00:10
-> [Help 1]
```

Then, do not worry. Delete the `debug.keystore` file that is located in `~/.android/`or `%USERPROFILE%\.android` folder. This may fix most of the cases; if it does not, do not panic. Had your Android SDK been installed in parallel with a former version, another `.\android\debug.keystore` file may remain there. Delete it and relaunch the build.

Integration with IDE

Unless weird exceptions arise, Maven features are fully integrated within the three major IDEs of the market: Eclipse, IntelliJ IDEA, and NetBeans. So, on this side, nothing special needs to be done. However, integrating Android SDK to the IDEs may need some additional operations.

Eclipse

In this section, we will go through the steps you need to follow in order to set up Maven and Android SDK to be used with Eclipse IDE. Some months ago, Eclipse was Google's first choice for creating the Android Studio but recently IntelliJ won the battle. Users that want to use Eclipse Luna for Android development need to follow some steps that we will describe in the following section.

Set up and integration of Maven and Android SDK

First of all, we need to manually install the Google plugin. Go to **Help | Install new software**. In the dialog that appears, enter the update site URL into the work with text box:

```
https://dl.google.com/eclipse/plugin/4.4
```

Add a name to remember the URL subscription and click **OK**. Then, wait for the list of modules to be retrieved. At the end, you should see something like the following screenshot:

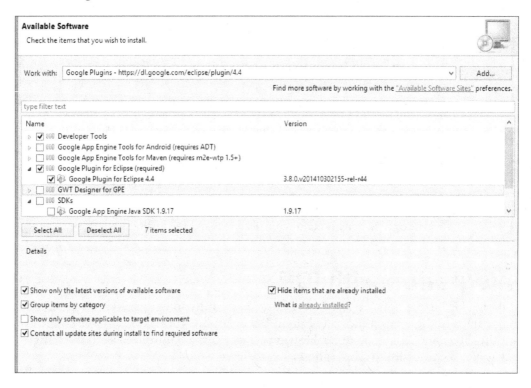

Check the boxes for the **Developer Tools** and the **Google Plugin for Eclipse** and then click on **Next** and finally accept the license agreement.

Then, set up the Android SDK: **Window** | **Preferences** | **Android** |. Browse to set the SDK Location field value | **OK**:

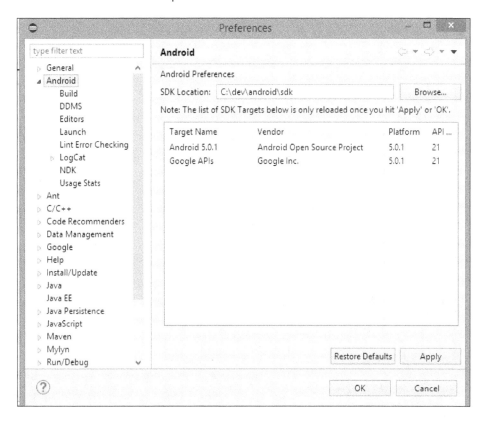

Besides, Eclipse embeds a built-in version of Maven (3.2.1 with Eclipse 4.4 Luna). Yet, you can use a specific version of Maven: go to **Window** | **Preferences** | **Maven** | **Installations** | **Add** and browse to the right location | **OK**, as shown in the following screenshot:

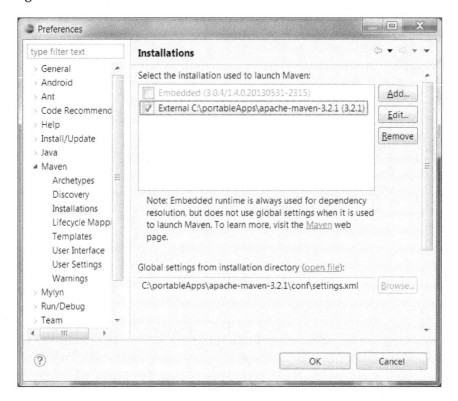

Creation of a project in Eclipse

Open **New** (*Alt+Shift+N*) | **Project** | **Maven** | **Maven Project**. Click **Next** on the first window that is displayed and you see the following screenshot:

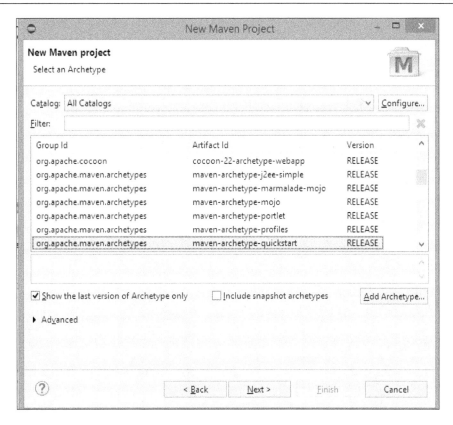

If you try to filter the catalog with the keyword "android", the list will probably show nothing; so, we need to add the archetype we want to use for the project creation. Click on the **Add Archetype** button and fill in the archetype details as shown in the next screenshot and click on the **OK** button:

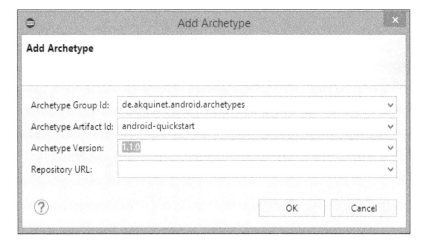

Now, the archetype should be available and selected in the dialog box we are looking at. Click again on **Next** and enter the same data we have specified to maven when we created the project using command line—see the following screenshot. Don't forget to change the platform property value to 21 as this is the SDK version we have installed so far. The default, which is 16, will cause the maven goals to fail because the corresponding SDK is not yet installed in our environment:

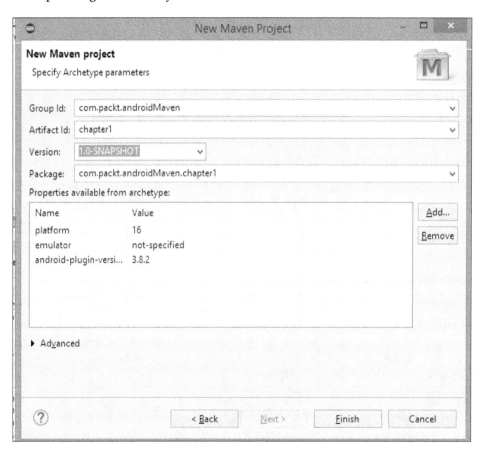

Now, you can open a terminal window and run the following command:

```
mvn clean install
```

You can also run the same goal using Eclipse and that's all. We have achieved the same result using our favorite IDE with just a few steps and we are now ready to start developing, testing, and running our first android application with Maven.

IntelliJ IDEA / Android Studio

IntelliJ IDEA is an IDE designed for Java development.

Set up and integration of Maven and Android SDK

Android Studio is promoted by Google as IDE for Android projects. Actually, Android Studio can be seen as a fork of main IntelliJ IDEA tool. Therefore, installation and configuration for both of them looks very similar or identical.

For pure Android projects, IntelliJ IDEA Community is sufficient: it includes core features such as Maven, Git, and Android support. Anyway, if you intend to develop enterprise projects linked with other Java/JEE frameworks and multitier architecture, you should consider installing the Ultimate version. Besides, beware that, at least so far, Android Studio is proposed as the suggested IDE from Google to develop Android applications.

Download IntelliJ IDEA from the page http://www.jetbrains.com/idea/ download/ and/or Android Studio from this one: https://developer.android. com/sdk/index.html

On first launch, IntelliJ IDEA and Android Studio will ask you whether you already have an install. If you do, then hint at the location of the settings as shown in the following screenshot:

Of course, settings of an IntelliJ IDEA install can be used for Android Studio and vice versa. The next steps of setup differ for IntelliJ IDEA and Android Studio.

Specific to Android Studio

Go to the settings (*Ctrl+Alt+S*) and then **Plugins**. Verify that the Maven plugins are installed.

Unlike, *do uncheck* **Gradle** plugin as shown in the following screenshot:

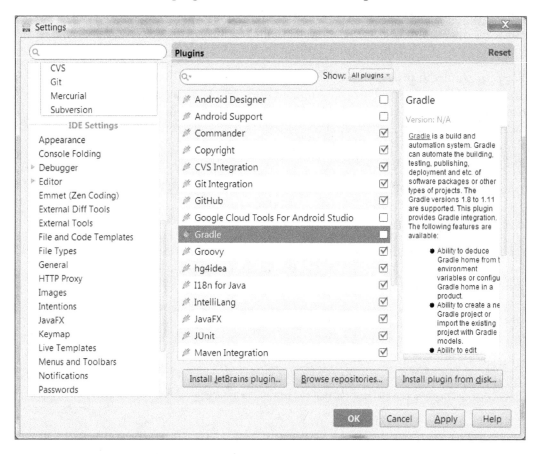

One might wonder why we need to disable Gradle to support Maven for Android development? Actually, by default, Android Studio considers Android/Maven projects as Eclipse-Android projects that are to be imported as regular Eclipse projects and then migrated to Gradle. This is the reason why we need to disable Gradle. Yet, this disables Android support, too. Don't worry, we will restore it later.

Besides, Android Studio should retrieve the Maven install location (based on the environment variable M2_HOME). If it does not, or if you need to use a custom location or version, you can navigate to **Maven** submenu inside the the settings (*Ctrl+Alt+S*) and override locations for Maven install, settings, and repository as shown in the following screenshot:

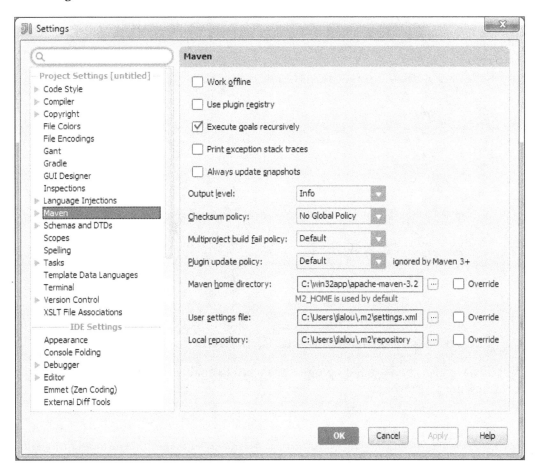

Specific to IntelliJ IDEA

On installing IntelliJ IDEA with the configuration wizard, take care to add Android and Maven plugins as shown in the following screenshot:

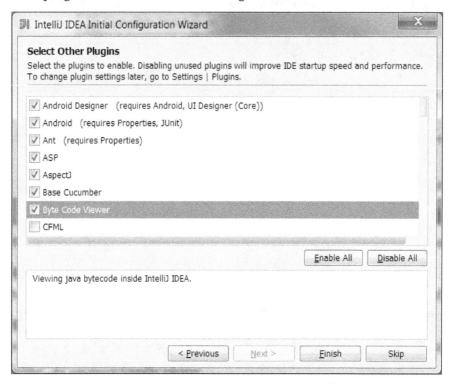

Post this, we also choose which plugins we want to enable or disable, as shown in the following screenshot:

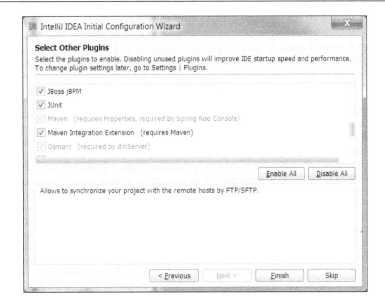

Import of project

Importing the project with Android Studio requires a bit more work than with pure IntelliJ IDEA.

Specific to Android Studio

We will follow the following steps to import an existing Android Maven project to Android Studio and use this as our IDE to further development as follows:

1. Go to **File | Import Project** as shown in the following screenshot:

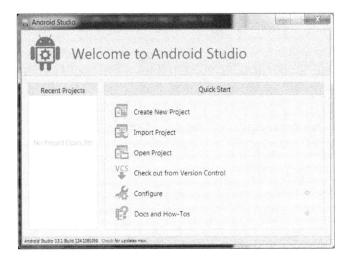

2. Browse to the POM and select it. Click on **OK**. Accept default options:

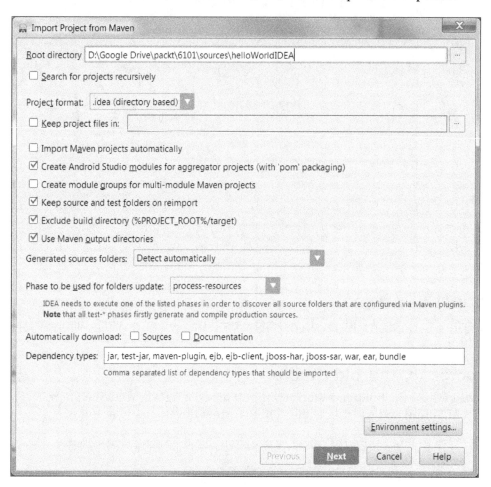

3. Confirm default options until **Finish** button. Android Studio displays the imported project, which is considered for the moment as a mere Java project, without any Android-specifics.

4. Go to the settings (*Ctrl+Alt+S*) | **Plugins**, restore the disabled plugins: **Android Designer**, **Android Support**, **Google Cloud Tools for Android Studio,** and **Gradle**.

5. Restart Android Studio. The IDE informs you that the Android framework is detected. Click on **Configure** as shown in the following screenshot:

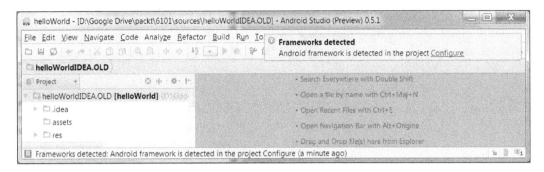

6. Check **AndroidManifest.xml** option and then click on **OK**:

7. Open the project structure (*Ctrl+Alt+Shift+S*) | **SDKs**. Click on the **+** sign (shortcut: *Alt+Insert*) | **Add a new SDK** | Select **Android SDK** | Browse to ANDROID_HOME variable | **OK** | Confirm both **Java SDK** and **Build target** | **OK**:

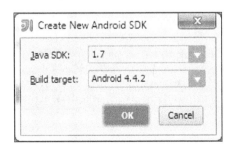

You can run Maven to build the project from Android Studio. You are now ready to develop!

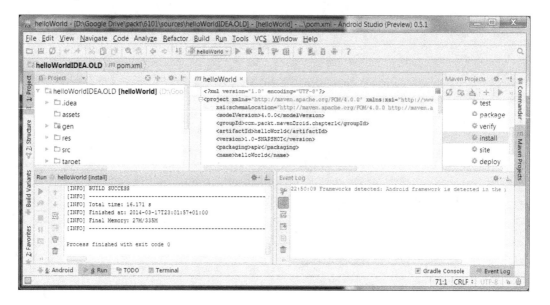

Specific to IntelliJ IDEA

Actually, IntelliJ IDEA is not as strongly linked to Gradle as Android Studio. This is why, for IntelliJ IDEA, the import follows the same template but is faster: simply import the POM and add the Android SDK.

NetBeans

NetBeans is the third commonly used IDE in Java development community. Originally maintained and promoted by Sun, now a division of Oracle, NetBeans still has features that fits the needs of Android development.

Download NetBeans from `https://netbeans.org/downloads/`. Install it.

Set up and integration of Maven and Android SDK

Let's start the setup by following these steps:

1. Go to **Tools | Plugins**. In the fourth tab ,that is, **Installed**, check whether Maven plugin is installed. If needed, install or update it as shown in the following screenshot:

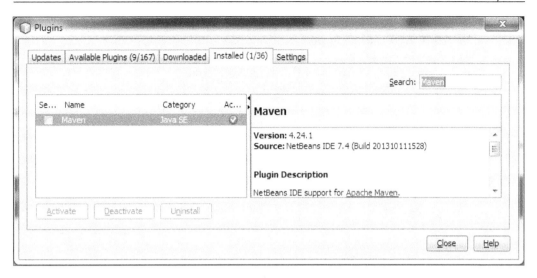

2. Like Eclipse, a default version of Maven is embedded; yet, you can override it: **Tools | Options | Java | Maven | Executions | Maven Home**.

   Android plugin for NetBeans is NBAndroid. It is not available through default update centers. Besides, the features of free version are poor and limited. Anyway, a 1-month evaluation plan is offered.

3. Go to **Settings** tab. Add and enter the name and URL, respectively, NBAndroid and `http://nbandroid.org/updates/updates.xml`, as shown in the following screenshot:

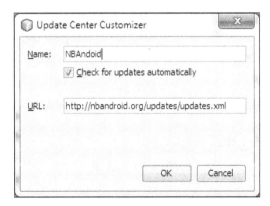

4. Go to **Available Plugins**, check **Android** and **NBAndroid Extensions** (**NBAndroid Gradle Support** is not needed, unless you think of using both Maven and Gradle), and then **Install**. Accept the license, dismiss the warning about nonsigned modules, and restart NetBeans.

5. Go to **Tools** | **Options** | **Miscellaneous** | **Android** | set Android SDK location as shown in the following screenshot:

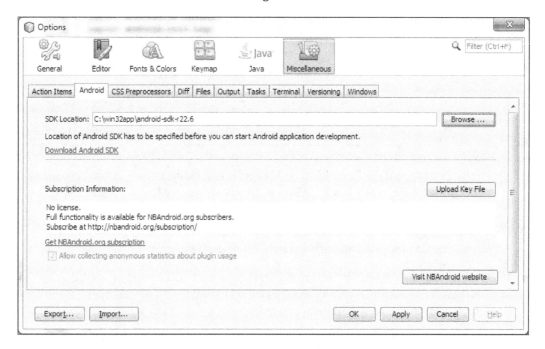

Import a project

Go to **File** | **Open Project** (*Ctrl+Shift+O*), browse until the folder containing the POM. You are ready to develop with Android.

Summary

Thus, in this opening chapter, we learned or revised how to install Maven and the Android SDK, and integrate them with an IDE. By now, you should be able to:

- Set up the JDK
- Set up Maven
- Set up Android SDK
- Set up a development environment
- Importing any Android project into major IDEs based on Maven

The next chapter will teach you the basic steps to develop a simple Android application using maven and so will use most of the things we discussed. If you don't feel confident in your current knowledge, then feel free to read this chapter again.

2
Starting the Development Phase

In the previous chapter, we saw how to install a complete work area to develop an Android application, using Maven as the build and project management tool. In this chapter we will see how to take advantage of Maven during the development phase.

Reminders about Android projects

Before diving deeper into the subject, let's review some concepts and rules related to Android.

At first glance, an Android project looks like any other Java project. Yet, some differences are fundamental.

An Android project is made of sources (Java, XML, and property files) and code that is generated by the system. All of these are compiled into bytecode and compressed as an **Android PacKage (APK)** file. Some Android projects also can produce AAR files but we will have the chance to learn more about this in a following chapter.

Let's open the Android project we have created in the previous chapter, using an artifact. As seen, the hierarchy of folders and files is as following:

- `assets/`: This will be reviewed later.
- `res/`: This is a set of resources.
    - `res/drawable-*pi/*.png`: Due to the strong fractionation of Android system, and the high variety of devices, resources such as pictures, fonts, and so on have to be taken into account while releasing. Unless you do limit the portability of your application, you have no choice but to adapt your resources to the largest audience.

○   `res/layout/activity_main.xml`: This file describes the widgets; that is, the basic or complex graphical components and their position, padding, and so on. Keep in mind, however, that most Android projects have more than one activity. In this case, this folder will contain information for each activity: you can consider each activity as being a screen. The following code snippet shows the contents of the `activity_main.xml` file:

```xml
<RelativeLayout
xmlns:android="http://schemas.android.com/apk/res/android"
    android:layout_width="match_parent"
    android:layout_height="match_parent"
    android:paddingBottom="@dimen/activity_vertical_margin"
    android:paddingLeft="@dimen/activity_horizontal_margin"
    android:paddingRight=
    "@dimen/activity_horizontal_margin"
    android:paddingTop="@dimen/activity_vertical_margin">
    <TextView
        android:layout_width="wrap_content"
        android:layout_height="wrap_content"
        android:text="@string/hello_world"/>
</RelativeLayout>
```

○   `res/menu/main.xml`: This is the entry point of the application. It looks like any other XML file in `res/layout/` folder but there is a big difference. This file is intended for use with a `menuInflater` parameter to create a menu in the `onCreateOptionsMenu` method of your activity.

○   `res/values*`: These files gather constants, such as strings, themes, and so on.

- `src/main/java`: Here is the folder for Java code specific to the application.

- `target/generated-sources/r`: This folder contains the Java code generated based on the different files as described in the preceding text. Notice this folder location is specific to projects built with Maven: by default, any IDE should create a `gen/` folder at the root of the project. To be even more accurate, this folder and its content are generated by Maven when goal `android:generate-source` method is executed.

- On root.

    ○   `AndroidManifest.xml`: This file summarizes different parameters, such as the **Software Development Kit (SDK)** needed to compile and/or to run the list of activities (among which the default activity), the rights needed by this application:

```xml
<?xml version="1.0" encoding="utf-8"?>
<manifest
xmlns:android="http://schemas.android.com/apk/res/android"
```

```
       package="com.packt.androidMaven"
       android:versionCode="1"
       android:versionName="1.0-SNAPSHOT">

         <uses-sdk
           android:minSdkVersion="8"
           android:targetSdkVersion="21"/>

       <application
         android:allowBackup="true"
         android:icon="@drawable/ic_launcher"
         android:label="@string/app_name"
         android:theme="@style/AppTheme">
         <activity android:name=".HelloAndroidActivity">
           <intent-filter>
             <action
             android:name="android.intent.action.MAIN"/>
             <category android:name="android.intent.category.
             LAUNCHER"/>
           </intent-filter>
         </activity>
       </application>
     </manifest>
```

- ° `default.properties`: The file used by Eclipse to determine the target system. If you don't see this in your local environment and you're not using Eclipse, then this is fine.

Now, let's review our POM and add some comments.

The headers are classic: they allow to determine the unique way to characterize our artifact, thanks to the triplet `groupId`, `artifactId`, `version` parameters such as shown in the following code snippet:

```
<?xml version="1.0" encoding="UTF-8"?>
<project xmlns="http://maven.apache.org/POM/4.0.0"
xmlns:xsi="http://www.w3.org/2001/XMLSchema-instance"
  xsi:schemaLocation="http://maven.apache.org/POM/4.0.0
  http://maven.apache.org/maven-v4_0_0.xsd">
  <modelVersion>4.0.0</modelVersion>
  <groupId>com.packt.androidMaven</groupId>
  <artifactId>chapter1</artifactId>
  <version>1.0-SNAPSHOT</version>
  <name>chapter1</name>
```

The sole difference, compared to other Java project, is the packaging: here, our archive is neither a "jar" nor an "ejb" or a "war" files, but the Android specific format: APK:

```
<packaging>apk</packaging>
```

The next block is made of properties. This corresponds to a good practice to factorize constants, version numbers, and so on in a unique location, so as to limit and avoid conflicts of versions:

```
<properties>
  <project.build.sourceEncoding>UTF-8</project.build.sourceEncoding>
  <platform.version>5.0.1_r2</platform.version>
  <android.plugin.version>3.8.2</android.plugin.version>
</properties>
```

A block `dependencies` lists the dependencies of our project. So far, we depend only on Android jar. The interesting point is that the dependency to Android jar is of scope `provided`. Therefore (and logically), the Android jar will not be included in the APK at the end of the compile because the intent is that the code will be run within a specific environment (device or emulator) where the `android.jar` file is expected to be in the classpath:

```
<dependencies>
  <dependency>
    <groupId>com.google.android</groupId>
    <artifactId>android</artifactId>
    <version>${platform.version}</version>
    <scope>provided</scope>
  </dependency>
</dependencies>
```

At last, the `build` block references the Maven plugin for Android. This will be explored later.

You can add the following block in your `settings.xml` file, available in `$M2_HOME/conf` or `~/.m2` location:

```
<pluginGroups>
  <pluginGroup>
    com.jayway.maven.plugins.android.generation2
  </pluginGroup>
</pluginGroups>
```

Then, you will be able to call the plugin without writing the full qualified name (`com.jayway.maven.plugins.android.generation2:android-maven-plugin`).

Creating an AVD

Before running any application, you have to create an **Android Virtual Device** (**AVD**), a kind of software emulator for Android device. Alternatively, you can run directly on a physical device (phone, tablet, and watch), which is actually faster. However, creating AVD instances allows you to test your application in a variety of configurations (OS version, screen size, memory, and so on) which is almost impossible to do with real devices. You can perform this operation via the **Graphical User Interface** (GUI), or in command line. Both produce the same result.

With the GUI

To run the AVD Manager in windows, you need to execute the AVD Manager.exe file located in the $ANDROID_HOME root; Linux users need to navigate to their SDK's tools/ directory and execute:

```
$ android avd
```

When you see the dialog—the list probably contains no emulators – click on **New** to add a new AVD. Fill out the fields relating to the device you want to emulate, as shown in the following screenshot:

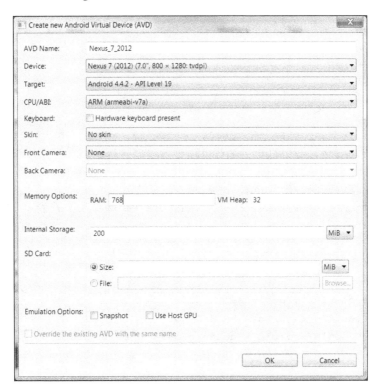

A pop up will confirm the result and the details of the device.

> By default, the AVD are stored in ~/.android/avd or %USERPROFILE%\.android\avd location. You can override this location by adding an environment variable named **ANDROID_SDK_HOME**, pointing to $ANDROID_HOME/.android for instance. Beware that AVD Manager will not create this folder if it does not yet exist; you have to create this folder before running AVD Manager!

In-command line

To create an AVD in-command line, you have to determine the list of AVD you can create owing to the configuration and content of your SDK.

Run the following command:

```
%ANDROID_HOME%\tools\android list target
```

You get the following output (only the first target is printed, as well as the headers of the others):

```
Available Android targets:
----------
id: 1 or "android-21"
    Name: Android 5.0.1
    Type: Platform
    API level: 21
    Revision: 2
        Skins: HVGA, QVGA, WQVGA400, WQVGA432, WSVGA, WVGA800
(default), WVGA854, WXGA720, WXGA800, WXGA800-7in, AndroidWearRound,
AndroidWearS
quare, AndroidWearRound, AndroidWearSquare
  Tag/ABIs : android-tv/armeabi-v7a, android-tv/x86, android-
wear/armeabi-v7a, android-wear/x86, default/armeabi-v7a, default/x86,
default/x8
6_64
----------
id: 2 or "Google Inc.:Google APIs :21"
The general pattern to create an AVD is:
$ANDROID_HOME/tools/android --name <name> --target <target> [options]
```

The target with `id 1` parameter corresponds to the platform `android-21`, and the default skin is `WVGA800`. So, to create the same AVD as in the preceding output, the command line will be as follows:

```
$ANDROID_HOME/tools/android create avd --name Nexus_7_2012 \
      --target "android-21" \
      --skin WVGA800 \
      --abi default/armeabi-v7a \
--path ~/.android/avd/Nexus_7_2012
```

Or, in short notation and default values:

```
$ANDROID_HOME/tools/android create avd -n Nexus_7_2012 \
      -t 1 \
      -b default/armeabi-v7a
```

The system confirms the creation of the AVD:

```
Android 5.0.1 is a basic Android platform.
Do you wish to create a custom hardware profile [no]
Created AVD 'Nexus_7_2012' based on Android 5.0.1, ARM (armeabi-v7a)
processor,
with the following hardware config:
hw.lcd.density=240
hw.ramSize=512
vm.heapSize=48
```

Nonetheless, this command-line-created AVD differs from the one created via the GUI, on the RAM size and heap size. You can edit the `config.ini` file within the folder where the AVD is stored (by default, in a subfolder of `~/.android/avd/`), and manually change these settings (as well as many others):

```
avd.ini.encoding=ISO-8859-1
abi.type=armeabi-v7a
hw.cpu.arch=arm
hw.cpu.model=cortex-a8
hw.lcd.density=240
hw.ramSize=512
image.sysdir.1=system-images\android-21\default\armeabi-v7a\
skin.name=WVGA800
skin.path=platforms\android-21\skins\WVGA800
tag.display=Default
tag.id=default
vm.heapSize=48
```

If you have to create multiple AVD with specific RAM and heap sizes, you can straightly edit the template, which is located in the skin you have chosen from the folder, for example, `$ANDROID_HOME/platforms/android-19/skins/WVGA800/hardware.ini`.

You can print a list of the installed AVDs by running the command:

```
$ANDROID_HOME/tools/android list avd
```

The expected output contains:

```
Available Android Virtual Devices:
    Name: Nexus_7_2012
    Path: C:\Users\jlalou\.android\avd\Nexus_7_2012.avd
  Target: Android 5.0.1 (API level 21)
 Tag/ABI: default/armeabi-v7a
    Skin: WVGA800
```

If you get such an error:

```
Error: Unable to find a 'userdata.img' file for ABI
default/armeabi-v7a to copy into the AVD folder.
```

Then, check if the file `%ANDROID_HOME%\system-images\android-19\default\armeabi-v7a\userdata.img` does exist. If this does, this may be related to a known issue on certain versions of the SDK. The best to do is to update the SDK.

You can also rename, move, and delete AVD with the three command lines, respectively:

```
$ANDROID_HOME//tools/android move avd --name Nexus_7_2012 --rename
Nexus_7_2012_bis
AVD 'Nexus_7_2012' moved.
```

```
$ANDROID_HOME/tools/android move avd --name Nexus_7_2012_bis --path
$ANDROID_HOME/tmp
AVD 'Nexus_7_2012_bis' moved.
```

```
$ANDROID_HOME/tools/android delete avd --name Nexus_7_2012_bis
Deleting file ....\avd\Nexus_7_2012_bis.ini
Deleting folder ...android-sdk-r22.6\tmp

AVD 'Nexus_7_2012_bis' deleted.
```

Develop and Build

Now that we have learned how to manage emulators and we have understood the typical Maven project structure and the basic configuration settings found in `pom.xml` file, we are ready to start developing our simple application. Remember that this book's purpose is not to teach how to code in Android SDK, but to explain how you can effectively use maven to speed up the development process. We will explain the required Maven commands but we will not focus on a particular IDE. Each IDE has its own way of creating Maven command executions and it's out of the scope of this book. You can experiment with your favorite IDE but in any case, if you want to master Android Maven development you should be able to at least run all Maven commands from a terminal window, like that discussed in the following sections and throughout this whole book.

Cleaning

Our first step is to clean the project from any generated source code or other artifacts. Typically, the Maven `clean` goal is included among any other target command, but for clarity, since it's the first time we explain this, we will run separate commands. During the next chapters, you will notice that the `clean` goal is executed with other Maven goals. Open a terminal window and navigate to the root of our example project. Then, run the following command:

```
mvn clean
```

Generating sources

Run `mvn android:generate-sources` command. Have a look at the expected output:

```
[INFO] Scanning for projects...
[INFO]
[INFO] -------------------------------------------------------------
------
[INFO] Building chapter1 1.0-SNAPSHOT
[INFO] -------------------------------------------------------------
------
[INFO]
[INFO] --- android-maven-plugin:3.8.2:generate-sources (default-cli) @
chapter1 ---
[INFO] ANDROID-904-002: Found aidl files: Count = 0
[INFO] ANDROID-904-002: Found aidl files: Count = 0
[INFO] Manifest merging disabled. Using project manifest only
[INFO] C:\dev\android\sdk\build-tools\21.1.2\aapt.exe [package, -f, -
```

```
-no-crunch, -I, C:\dev\android\sdk\platforms\android-21\android.jar,
-M, C:\dev\android\packt\BookSteps\chapter1\AndroidManifest.xml, -S,
C:\dev\android\packt\BookSteps\chapter1\res, -A,
C:\dev\android\packt\BookSteps\chapter1\target\generated-sources\
combined-assets\assets, -m,
-J, C:\dev\android\packt\BookSteps\chapter1\target\generated-
sources\r,
--output-text-symbols, C:\dev\android\packt\BookSteps\chapter1\target,
--auto-add-overlay]
[INFO] ------------------------------------------------------------
------
[INFO] BUILD SUCCESS
[INFO] ------------------------------------------------------------
------
[INFO] Total time: 1.709 s
[INFO] Finished at: 2015-01-18T18:23:01+02:00
[INFO] Final Memory: 13M/310M
[INFO] ------------------------------------------------------------
----------
```

Basically, as hinted, `android:generate-sources` goal calls the `aapt` tool from the Android SDK.

As expected, a `target/generated-sources` file has been created. It contains the regular files already seen in the preceding text, such as the `R.java` file.

Build

To build with Maven, simply run `mvn clean install`.

This compiles the project and generates several artifacts under target directory:

- `classes.dex`: This archive gathers the compressed bytecote generated by compilation, in a format understandable by **Dalvik**, which is the Java Virtual Machine executed below Android system. Actually, Dalvik is quite more limited than **HotSpot** or **JRockit** (the major JVM in desktop computers and servers), but is more adapted to short-resource devices such as smartphones and tablets.

- `{artifactId}.ap_`: This archive gathers the resources of the application: XML, picture files, and so on.

- `{artifactId}.apk`: This Android PacKage, compressed and signed. Basically, the APK file merges the `{artifactId}.ap_` and `classes.dex` files.

- `{artifactId}.jar`: A Java archive containing zipped bytecode (`.class` files).

Actually, in the operation of building, our aim is to get an APK file; therefore, running another goal such as `mvn clean android:apk` may have obtained the same result.

Emulator

You can start and stop one or many emulators with Maven commands:

Start

`mvn android:emulator-start` starts up an AVD. By default, Maven searches for an AVD named `Default`. This can be overridden via changing some options:

- Either in the POM: add a block similar to:

```
<plugin>
  <groupId>com.jayway.maven.plugins.android.generation2</groupId>
    <artifactId>android-maven-plugin</artifactId>
    <version>${android.plugin.version}</version>
    <extensions>true</extensions>
    <configuration>
      <sdk>
        <platform>21</platform>
      </sdk>
      <emulator>
        <!--Name of the AVD to start/stop-->
        <avd>Nexus_7_2012</avd>
        <!-- Timeout to consider whether or not the AVD is
        successful or failed. Do not be stingy on this value,
        since your material configuration may affect and influence
        on startup speed-->
        <wait>30000</wait>
        <!-- Any other option-->
        <options></options>
      </emulator>
    </configuration>
</plugin>
```

- In the command line:

```
mvn android:emulator-start -Dandroid.emulator.avd=Nexus_7_2012 \
-Dandroid.emulator.wait=30000 \
-Dandroid.emulator.options=-no-skin
```

The options available are those of `$ANDROID_HOME/tools/emulator`: you can display them by running `$ANDROID_HOME/tools/emulator –help`, or, alternatively, by consulting this Gist: `https://gist.github.com/JonathanLalou/180c87554d82 78b0e6d7`

The expected output is like:

```
[INFO] ----------------------------------------------------------------
-------
[INFO] Building chapter1 1.0-SNAPSHOT
[INFO] ----------------------------------------------------------------
------
[INFO]
[INFO] --- android-maven-plugin:3.8.2:emulator-start (default-cli) @
helloWorld ---
[INFO] Android emulator command: ""C:\win32app\android-sdk-r22.6\tools\
emulator"" -avd Nexus_7_2012

[INFO] Found 0 devices connected with the Android Debug Bridge
[INFO] Starting android emulator with script: C:\Users\jlalou\AppData\
Local\Temp\ConsolePortableTemp\\android-maven-plugin-emulator-start.vbs
[INFO] Waiting for emulator start:300000
[INFO] Emulator is up and running.
```

Actually, under Windows the plugin only calls a VB script to launch the emulator.

Stop

`mvn android:emulator-stop` stops up an AVD. By default, Maven searches for an AVD named `Default`. Like `emulator-start` goal, this default behavior can be overridden if the POM contains a `<configuration>` block pointing at the AVD, or if the command line includes the option `-Dandroid.emulator.avd=<name_of_ the_AVD>`

Stop all

`mvn android:emulator-stop` stops all AVD running on the system.

Deploy

With Maven, provided that you have already built the project through `mvn clean install`, run the command:

`mvn android:deploy.`

This output is similar to:

```
[INFO] --- android-maven-plugin:3.8.2:deploy (default-cli) @
helloWorld ---
[INFO] Waiting for initial device list from the Android Debug Bridge
[INFO] Found 1 devices connected with the Android Debug Bridge
[INFO] android.device parameter not set, using all attached devices
[INFO] Emulator emulator-5554_Nexus_7_2012_unknown_sdk found.
[INFO] emulator-5554_Nexus_7_2012_unknown_sdk :    Successfully
installed C:\Users\jlalou\==PRIVATE==\GDrive\packt\6101\sources\
helloWorldWithoutIDEA\target\chapter1.apk to emulator-5554_Nexus_7_2012_
unknown_sdk
```

Then, in the emulator, the APK that you have compiled and deployed appears in the application list (as shown in the following screenshot: fourth line, second column):

By default, Maven deploys the application on all active emulators; to deploy on a single target, add the `-Dandroid.device=<name_of_the_AVD>` parameter, as given here:

```
mvn android:deploy -Dandroid.device=Nexus_7_2012
[INFO] --- android-maven-plugin:3.8.2:deploy (default-cli) @
AndroidTier ---
[INFO] Waiting for initial device list from the Android Debug Bridge
[INFO] Found 1 devices connected with the Android Debug Bridge
[INFO] android.device parameter set to Nexus_7_2012
[INFO] emulator-5554_Nexus_7_2012_unknown_sdk :    Successfully
installed C:\Users\jlalou\==PRIVATE==\GDrive\packt\6101\sources\
helloWorldWithoutIDEA\target\chapter1.apk to emulator-5554_Nexus_7_2012_
unknown_sdk
```

Undeploy

To undeploy the application, run:

```
mvn android:undeploy
```

The output contains:

```
[INFO] --- android-maven-plugin:3.8.2:undeploy (default-cli) @
helloWorld ---
[INFO] Waiting for initial device list from the Android Debug Bridge
[INFO] Found 1 devices connected with the Android Debug Bridge
[INFO] android.device parameter not set, using all attached devices
[INFO] Emulator emulator-5554_Nexus_7_2012_unknown_sdk found.
[INFO] emulator-5554_Nexus_7_2012_unknown_sdk :    Successfully
uninstalled com.packt.mavenDroid.chapter1 from emulator-
5554_Nexus_7_2012_unknown_sdk
```

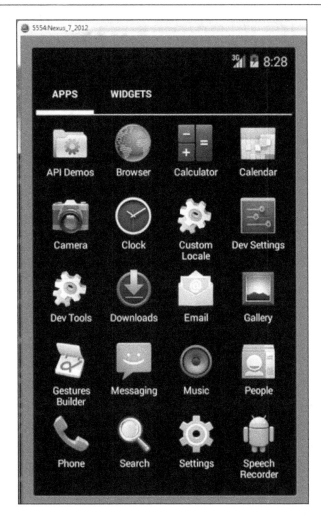

The application does not appear anymore.

At this point, you may not be convinced of the advantage of such goals. Anyway, step back and think of the industrialization of deployments and tests on a great diversity of devices.

Architecture principles

Now that we are able to build and deploy on an AVD, let's resume the development phase itself.

Standalone application

In "simple cases", the Android application has no contact with any other tier. The application is self-dependent. Therefore, the principles of architecture common to any other standalone application apply.

The application has to be divided based on functional criteria, for instance: domain or model, **Data Access Object (DAO)**, service, and view. In Android terminology, views are activities. A graph of direct dependencies is shown in the following image:

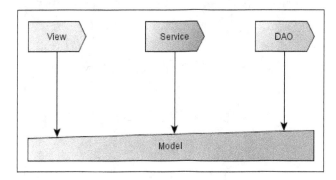

In other terms, the view may have direct access to the services, but not to the DAO layer. Yet, any layer is aware of the model.

This best practice allows developing many applications built on common basic blocks, with a frontend and a behavior being totally different.

The management of external dependencies is regular: dependencies are defined mainly by the triplet `groupId`, `artifactId`, and `version` parameters; the dependency scope can be `compile`, `provided`, `runtime`, or `system`. If your application depends on another Android application, do no forget that the dependency type is `apk`, and not `jar`.

Since you add external dependencies to your Android application project, you should get the following error, repeated as many times as inner or anonymous classes appear in your dependency graph:

```
[INFO] warning: Ignoring InnerClasses attribute for an
anonymous inner class
[INFO] (any.class.from.any.package) that doesn't come
with an
[INFO] associated EnclosingMethod attribute. This class
was probably produced by a
[INFO] compiler that did not target the modern .class
file format. The recommended
[INFO] solution is to recompile the class from source,
using an up-to-date compiler
[INFO] and without specifying any "-target" type
options. The consequence of ignoring
[INFO] this warning is that reflective operations on
this class will incorrectly
[INFO] indicate that it is *not* an inner class.
```

This error is not to worry about. If it does bore you, you can get the source code of the dependencies in the case of open source projects, and then include them in your own source code (anyway, beware of licenses such as **General Public License** (**GPL**) that may require you to make your application source code become GPL, too). More seriously, this problem means your project, or one of its dependencies or even sub-dependencies, requires Java 1.3 back-compatibility. As stated, you can ignore this warning.

As an example, let's consider the project com.packt.androidMaven.:sampleProject where you can download from here : https://github.com/ppapapetrou76/AndroidMavenDevelopment/tree/master/Chapter2. It is a regular project, with three submodules:

```
<modules>
    <module>model</module>
    <module>service</module>
    <module>AndroidTier</module>
</modules>
```

We haven't discussed Maven modules so far; so, it's a good idea to explain their purpose. The idea behind modules is to split a large project into smaller functional pieces of projects. Each module should have a concrete sets of responsibilities and low level module should not be dependent to high level modules. When Maven builds a multimodule project, it uses a mechanism that is called a reactor. Actually, here's what maven does:

- Collects all the available modules to build
- Sorts the projects into the correct build order
- Builds the selected projects in order

Our first module, `model`, consists of a single file, representing an entity `Book`, as a Java bean, with mere properties, getters and setters, and an overridden `toString()` method:

```
public class Book {
   private Integer id;
   private String title;
   private String format;
   private String color;
   private Integer numberOfPages;
   private Boolean brandNew;
   public Book() {
   }
   public String toString() {
     return "Book{" +
       "id=" + id +
       ", title='" + title + '\'' +
       ", format='" + format + '\'' +
       ", color='" + color + '\'' +
        ", numberOfPages=" + numberOfPages +
        ", brandNew=" + brandNew +
      '}';
   }
   // plus getters and setters
}
```

Module `service` depends only on `model` parameter:

```
<project xmlns:xsi="http://www.w3.org/2001/XMLSchema-instance"
   xmlns="http://maven.apache.org/POM/4.0.0"
   xsi:schemaLocation="http://maven.apache.org/POM/4.0.0
   http://maven.apache.org/maven-v4_0_0.xsd">
   <modelVersion>4.0.0</modelVersion>
```

```
<parent>
  <groupId>com.packt.androidMaven</groupId>
  <artifactId>sampleProject</artifactId>
  <version>1.0-SNAPSHOT</version>
</parent>
<artifactId>service</artifactId>
<version>${project.parent.version}</version>
<name>service</name>

<dependencies>
  <dependency>
    <groupId>${project.parent.groupId}</groupId>
    <artifactId>model</artifactId>
    <version>${project.parent.version}</version>
  </dependency>
</dependencies>
</project>
```

A service interface `BookService` is declared, with one method to implement:

```
Book createBook(String title, String format, String color, Integer
numberOfPages);
```

The implementation creates an instance of `Book` class:

```
public class BookServiceImpl implements BookService {
  @Override
  public Book createBook(String title, String format, String
  color, Integer numberOfPages) {
    final Book book = new Book();
    book.setTitle(title);
    book.setFormat(format);
    book.setColor(color);
    book.setNumberOfPages(numberOfPages);
    return book;
  }
}
```

The Android application, `com.packt.androidMaven:AndroidTier`, depends on `model` and `service` parameter. We may have not declared the dependency on `model` parameter, because of the transitive and implicit dependencies induced because of `service`. Besides, the Android application obviously depends on `com.google.android:android` jar:

```
<dependencies>
  <dependency>
```

```
        <groupId>com.google.android</groupId>
        <artifactId>android</artifactId>
        <version>${platform.version}</version>
        <scope>provided</scope>
    </dependency>
    <dependency>
      <!--Add a dependency on 'model' -->
      <groupId>${project.groupId}</groupId>
      <artifactId>model</artifactId>
    <version>${project.version}</version>
    </dependency>
    <!--Add a dependency on 'service' -->
    <dependency>
        <groupId>${project.groupId}</groupId>
        <artifactId>service</artifactId>
        <version>${project.version}</version>
    </dependency>
  </dependencies>
```

The Android application consists of a single activity, calling the service and displaying the result:

```
public void onCreate(Bundle savedInstanceState) {
   super.onCreate(savedInstanceState);
   final TextView textview;
   final Book book;
   book = bookService.createBook("Maven and Android", "eBook",
   "black", 150);
   textview = new TextView(this);
   textview.setText(book.toString());
   setContentView(textview);
}
```

You can build the project from the parent POM folder:

`mvn clean install`

Then, go to `AndroidTier` module folder. Start up Android emulator and deploy the APK:

```
mvn android:emulator-start
mvn android:deploy
```

The result appears in the emulator as shown in the following screenshot:

Android application within an n-tier architecture

Standalone Android applications are more the exception than the rule: the trend for Android applications is to be part of two or three-tier architecture: this way, the Android application is only one view (among others), connected to one (or more) servers through HTTP (JSON or SOAP web services), linked to a backend such as a database, as shown in the following screenshot:

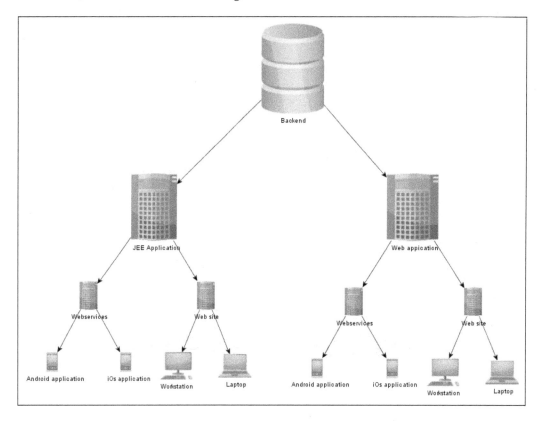

An Android application integrated within a larger project must follow the same rules as any other multi-tier project:

The Android application artifact should contain only the resource and source code specific to the application. In other terms, matching with **Model-View-Controller (MVC)** design pattern, concentrate the look and feel the information in the project that will generate the APK. Business treatments, common to the Android application and a web application for instance, must be factorized in a common business layer.

Many advantages and benefits result therefrom: first, the code is factorized. Second, you can move business intelligence and logic in a computer far more powerful than an Android device, which is, by definition, limited in CPU and RAM. Third, you protect your business algorithms from reverse-engineering: an Android APK, although encrypted and signed, remains breakable.

Android applications often are in dialog with a server. On development time, the emulator has to access the web server (in general, a servlet container such as **Tomcat** or **Jetty**) that is deployed on the same physical machine as the emulator. To access the local web server, getting *localhost* or *127.0.0.1* is not used: rather, use the IP *10.0.2.2* (do not forget the port number, such as the default *8080*) which is mapped to the *localhost* on which the emulator is running.

Another best practice is to expose the entities and interfaces needed by the Android application in a minimal set of dependencies.

In the following schema, the Android application depends only on an artifact named `contract`, gathering entities and declared service interfaces. You may notice that the service implementation web application artifacts also depend only on `contract` as well as on `dao`:

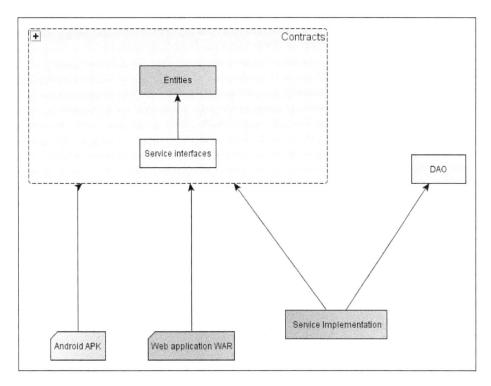

Here is how Maven manages such a situation:

The parent POM contains a `<packaging>pom</packaging>` tag and declares its submodules:

```
<modules>
  <module>entity</module>
  <module>service</module>
  <module>contract</module>
  <module>dao</module>
  <module>service-impl</module>
  <module>webtier</module>
  <module>AndroidTier</module>
</modules>
```

The `entity` parameter has no special dependency, unlike `service` parameter that depends on `entity` parameter.

`contract` declares itself as `pom`, and propagates the two dependencies onto `entity` and `service` parameters:

```
<?xml version="1.0" encoding="UTF-8"?>
<project xmlns="http://maven.apache.org/POM/4.0.0"
  xmlns:xsi="http://www.w3.org/2001/XMLSchema-instance"
  xsi:schemaLocation="http://maven.apache.org/POM/4.0.0
  http://maven.apache.org/xsd/maven-4.0.0.xsd">
  <modelVersion>4.0.0</modelVersion>
  <parent>
  <groupId>com.packt.androidMaven.chapter2</groupId>
  <artifactId>multitiers</artifactId>
  <version>1.0-SNAPSHOT</version>
  </parent>
  <packaging>pom</packaging>
  <artifactId>contract</artifactId>
  <version>1.0-SNAPSHOT</version>
  <!-- This POM declares and propagates two dependencies -->
  <dependencies>
    <dependency>
      <groupId>com.packt.androidMaven.chapter2</groupId>
      <artifactId>entity</artifactId>
      <version>1.0-SNAPSHOT</version>
    </dependency>
    <dependency>
      <groupId>com.packt.androidMaven.chapter2</groupId>
      <artifactId>service</artifactId>
```

```
            <version>1.0-SNAPSHOT</version>
        </dependency>
    </dependencies>
</project>
```

`AndroidTier` and `webtier` parameters behave in a similar manner: they depend only on `contract`. `service-impl` declares a dependency on `dao` parameter in more of `contract` parameter. Beware! The dependency on the `contract` parameter must be declared with type `pom`:

```
<dependency>
    <groupId>${project.groupId}</groupId>
    <artifactId>contract</artifactId>
    <version>1.0-SNAPSHOT</version>
    <type>pom</type>
</dependency>
```

Android with dependencies on SDK Add-ons

You may need some dependencies, external of core Android, but yet linked to it. The most common case is when you depend on Google Maps. The JAR file of Google Maps is installed with the other add-ons by default install configuration.

If your project depends on Google Maps (or, similarly, to `usb` or `effects` JARs), firstly you have to install the dependencies in your local repository:

```
mvn install:install-file  \
-Dfile=%ANDROID_HOME%\add-ons\addon-google_apis-google-19\libs \
-DgroupId=com.google.android \
-DartifactId=maps \
-Dversion=19_r3   \
-Dpackaging=jar \
-DgeneratePom=true
```

Then, declare the dependency, specifying the scope as provided:

```
<dependency>
    <groupId>com.google.android.maps</groupId>
    <artifactId>maps</artifactId>
    <version>19_r3</version>
    <!-- the JAR is already available within the Android emulator or
    device ; no use to embed it within your application -->
    <scope>provided</scope>
</dependency>
```

The <version> tag of artifact maps differs from that of "Android core" JAR: *19_r3* versus *4.4.2_r3*. In other terms, for Android add-ons, the version to write follows the API level, whereas "Android core" follows the release version. In a further chapter, we will deal with maven-android-sdk-deployer plugin, which eases the installation process of Android dependencies.

Summary

Thus, in this second chapter, we learned or revised concepts related to Android SDK and tools. We reviewed how to create AVDs in the GUI and in the command line. We saw how to start/stop an emulator from Maven, and how to clean, build, deploy, and undeploy an APK onto an emulator. Finally, we described best practices in the architecture of Android projects managed by Maven.

In the next chapter, we will begin exploring unit testing.

3
Unit Testing

So far, we have discussed some fundamental steps needed for setting up your development environment and for creating a very simple Android application using Maven. We also saw how to manage Android emulators and run the application during development stages. In this chapter, we will cover the topic of unit testing. We will see the configuration needed for running unit tests using various frameworks and get reports about code coverage.

This and the subsequent chapter, will not teach you how to write tests for Android application, although there will be some minimal examples to demonstrate the material of each chapter. If you're not familiar with the concepts discussed in the next pages, you are strongly encouraged to read the resources that we will provide in each section.

Effectively testing Android applications

Before we start to discuss the essential Maven plugins to run Android application tests, it's important to review some good practices we should have in mind. In every software system, there are two generic types of testing: Unit Testing and Integration Testing. Each type has its own characteristics and targets on different goals. Let's quickly make their differences and their purposes clear:

- Unit testing focuses on ensuring that the individual units of source code are doing the things right. Such tests should run very fast, should not depend on each other or on any external resources, and should evaluate the expected output of the code under testing.

- Integration tests, on the other hand, can be slow and focus on testing software as an integrated system with external resources. In-container testing, database testing, or even UI testing fall into this category. For an Android application, the integration tests require the presence of a real device (phone, tablet, and so on) or an emulator.

As we will see in this chapter and the next one, it is not a good idea to mix the execution of unit and integration tests; so bear in mind that when talking of an Android application, unit tests usually test the business logic and the code of the activities as isolated entities, whereas integration testing ensures the behavior of the application from a user point of view. Now that we outlined the purpose of these testing types in an Android application context, it is time to start configuring our Maven project.

Running typical unit tests

From this chapter until the end of this book, we will use a sample project to demonstrate the topics we will cover. For this one, we will reuse the basic structure of the three-module (model, service, and AndroidTier) Maven project we introduced in *Chapter 2*, *Starting the Development Phase*, with some naming modifications, and we will build on top of this. The complete source code can be found on the following GitHub link `https://github.com/ppapapetrou76/AndroidMavenDevelopment/Chapter3`.

> Assume that you have a git client installed in your machine, you can clone the project locally by running the following command:
> `git clone https://github.com/ppapapetrou76/AndroidMavenDevelopment.`

Running our first unit test with Maven is easy. By default, Maven uses the `maven-surefire-plugin` command to execute unit tests for all files found under the `/src/test/java/` directory; so, we don't need to add any dependency to our `pom.xml` file. We need, however, to add a Maven dependency of the unit testing framework that we will use. JUnit and TestNG are the most popular unit testing frameworks for Java; so, we strongly advised to use one of them, as both of them are fully compatible with Android application development.

The business logic of the project is located in our service module; so, we need to add the following lines inside the `dependencies` tag of the corresponding `pom.xml` file.

For Junit (`http://junit.org`):

```
<dependency>
    <groupId>junit</groupId>
    <artifactId>junit</artifactId>
    <version>4.10</version>
    <scope>test</scope>
</dependency>
```

Although the latest JUnit version at the time this book was written was 4.11, we use 4.10 for avoiding some compatibility issues discovered when implementing the test cases of this and the following chapter.

For TestNG (`http://testng.org`):

```
<dependency>
    <groupId>org.testing</groupId>
    <artifactId>testing</artifactId>
    <version>6.8.8</version>
    <scope>test</scope>
</dependency>
```

 You have already noticed that we have defined the scope of the testing library dependency as `test`. This instructs Maven to use this dependency only when executing test-related phases and not include this when building the package.

Before we implement our first unit test and run it with Maven, let's have a look of the parent `pom.xml` file of our sample project:

```
<?xml version="1.0" encoding="UTF-8"?>
<project xmlns="http://maven.apache.org/POM/4.0.0"
xmlns:xsi="http://www.w3.org/2001/XMLSchema-instance"
xsi:schemaLocation="http://maven.apache.org/POM/4.0.0
http://maven.apache.org/maven-v4_0_0.xsd">
  <modelVersion>4.0.0</modelVersion>
  <groupId>com.packt.androidMaven</groupId>
  <artifactId>sampleProject</artifactId>
  <version>1.0-SNAPSHOT</version>
  <packaging>pom</packaging>
  <name>AndroidDevelopmentMaven</name>
  <description>Android App Development with Maven</description>

  <modules>
    <module>model</module>
    <module>service</module>
    <module>AndroidTier</module>
  </modules>
  <properties>
    <project.build.sourceEncoding>UTF-
    8</project.build.sourceEncoding>
    <platform.version>5.0.1_r2</platform.version>
    <android.plugin.version>3.8.2</android.plugin.version>
  </properties>
```

```
<build>
  <finalName>${project.artifactId}</finalName>
  <pluginManagement>
    <plugins>
      <plugin>
        <groupId>com.jayway.maven.plugins.android.generation2
        </groupId>
        <artifactId>android-maven-plugin</artifactId>
        <version>${android.plugin.version}</version>
        <extensions>true</extensions>
      </plugin>
    </plugins>
  </pluginManagement>
</build>
</project>
```

Accordingly, the pom.xml files of the three submodules have changed. Here's how the service module pom.xml file will look like after the addition of the JUnit dependency:

```
<?xml version="1.0" encoding="UTF-8"?>
<project xmlns="http://maven.apache.org/POM/4.0.0"
xmlns:xsi="http://www.w3.org/2001/XMLSchema-instance"
xsi:schemaLocation="http://maven.apache.org/POM/4.0.0
http://maven.apache.org/xsd/maven-4.0.0.xsd">
  <modelVersion>4.0.0</modelVersion>
  <parent>
    <groupId>com.packt.androidMaven</groupId>
    <artifactId>sampleProject</artifactId>
    <version>1.0-SNAPSHOT</version>
  </parent>
  <artifactId>service</artifactId>
  <packaging>jar</packaging>
  <dependencies>
    <dependency>
      <groupId>${project.parent.groupId}</groupId>
      <artifactId>model</artifactId>
      <version>${project.parent.version}</version>
    </dependency>
    <dependency>
      <groupId>junit</groupId>
      <artifactId>junit</artifactId>
      <version>4.10</version>
      <scope>test</scope>
```

```
      </dependency>
    </dependencies>
  </project>
```

Now, we can move forward and write a very simple unit test using the JUnit library. Normally, all known IDEs have plenty of utilities to quickly add unit test classes, but since this book is not IDE-specific, we will follow the generic way. Create a new class named `BookServiceImplTest` under the `/src/test/java/com/packt/androidmaven/service` directory and add the following code:

```
package com.packt.androidmaven.service;
import com.packt.androidmaven.model.Book;
import org.junit.Assert;
import org.junit.Test;
public class BookServiceImplTest {
  private final BookService bookService = new BookServiceImpl();
  private static final String TITLE = "Maven and Android";
  private static final String FORMAT = "eBook";
  private static final String COLOR = "Black";
  private static final Integer PAGES = 190;

  @Test
  public void should_create_book() {
    Book actualBook = bookService.createBook(TITLE, FORMAT, COLOR,
    PAGES);
    Assert.assertEquals(TITLE, actualBook.getTitle());
    Assert.assertEquals(FORMAT, actualBook.getFormat());
    Assert.assertEquals(COLOR, actualBook.getColor());
    Assert.assertEquals(PAGES, actualBook.getNumberOfPages());
    Assert.assertNull(actualBook.getId());
    Assert.assertNull(actualBook.isBrandNew());
  }
}
```

The next step is to execute the test we just implemented. First, navigate to the root directory of your project and run the following Maven command to compile and install all the artifacts produced by this project in the local Maven repository. We don't want to run the tests this time, and so we instruct Maven to skip them:

```
mvn clean install -DskipTests
```

After this we navigate to the service module directory, open a terminal, and run the following Maven command:

```
mvn clean test
```

The output should look similar to the following screenshot:

```
T E S T S
Running com.packt.androidmaven.service.BookServiceImplTest
Tests run: 1, Failures: 0, Errors: 0, Skipped: 0, Time elapsed: 0.032 sec

Results :

Tests run: 1, Failures: 0, Errors: 0, Skipped: 0

[INFO] -----------------------------------------------------------
[INFO] BUILD SUCCESS
[INFO] -----------------------------------------------------------
[INFO] Total time: 2.365 s
[INFO] Finished at: 2015-01-23T17:21:10+02:00
[INFO] Final Memory: 16M/246M
[INFO] -----------------------------------------------------------
```

You can create as many unit tests that are needed for the business logic of your application just like you're writing test for any java application and see their results by running the command we already described. Now, let's move on and discover the second important part of Android unit testing.

Unit testing of activities

Clearly, one of the most important parts of an Android application is the implementation of activities. Like we already discussed, all applications have activities, but only a few of them include domain models and business logic. The norm is to create applications that behave like clients of an existing backend system using web services.

There are two types of activities testing:

- **Unit testing**: Each activity is tested in isolation from the rest of the application. This type of testing focuses on the layout and the expected components.

- **Integration testing** (in Android, it's also called instrumentation): Each activity is tested as part of the overall application. This type of testing ensures that the activities are doing the right things on user behavior, such as opening new activities, displaying toast messages, and so on.

In this chapter, we are going to see how to use Maven to drive the unit testing of activities and part of the following chapter will discuss the instrumentation testing.

 Although we distinguish two types of activities testing, in practice both of them need an emulator to run. The reason why we call one of these types as 'Unit Testing' has to do with the fact that an activity is considered as the smallest unit of code in the Android context.

Before we discuss the necessary Maven configuration for running activity unit tests, we need to explain that Maven, although it is a great build tool, is not very clever in all cases. So, if you start writing activity unit tests in the same module that your unit tests are placed, it won't find any difference and will try to run all of them. But like we mentioned before, activities unit tests need an emulator; therefore, they will fail and most probably we will see an error message about using stubs.

To overcome this issue, we create a new Maven module and we place all of our tests inside the /src/test/java/ folder. Let's see the steps we need to create this module and run our first activity unit test.

Creating a dedicated unit testing module

We open a terminal and navigate to the root folder of the application. Then, we type the following commands to create a new module:

```
mvn archetype:generate \
  -DarchetypeArtifactId=android-quickstart \
  -DarchetypeGroupId=de.akquinet.android.archetypes \
  -DarchetypeVersion=1.1.0 \
  -DgroupId=com.packt.androidMaven \
  -DartifactId=AndroidUnitTests \
  -Dversion=1.0-SNAPSHOT \
  -Dplatform=21 \
  --batch-mode \
```

To verify that the new module was correctly generated, first ensure that a folder named AndroidUnitTests was created under the root folder of our project. Then, open our parent pom.xml file. Locate the <modules> tag and check that a new entry <module>AndroidUnitTests</module> has been added. We need to also change (or add it if it is not there) the <packaging> tag to the value of apk. Our next step is to add the dependency of the actual Android application module in the pom.xml file of our new module. It is required that we define it as a 'jar' dependency so that we can invoke R. references in our tests.

 R is the class containing the definitions for all resources of your packaged application. You can consider it as the namespace of your application; so, if in our case since manifest package name is com.packt.androidMaven, the R class will be generated with the symbols of all our resources in this class: com.packt.androidMaven.R

Finally, we need to add a test library (android-test) provided by an Android that will help us write android-oriented unit tests. Here is the final version of our new module's `pom.xml` file:

```xml
<?xml version="1.0" encoding="UTF-8"?>
<project xmlns="http://maven.apache.org/POM/4.0.0"
xmlns:xsi="http://www.w3.org/2001/XMLSchema-instance"
xsi:schemaLocation="http://maven.apache.org/POM/4.0.0
http://maven.apache.org/xsd/maven-4.0.0.xsd">
  <modelVersion>4.0.0</modelVersion>
  <parent>
    <groupId>com.packt.androidMaven</groupId>
    <artifactId>sampleProject</artifactId>
    <version>1.0-SNAPSHOT</version>
  </parent>
  <artifactId>AndroidUnitTests</artifactId>
  <packaging>apk</packaging>

  <dependencies>
    <dependency>
      <groupId>com.packt.androidMaven</groupId>
      <artifactId>AndroidTier</artifactId>
      <version>${project.version}</version>
      <scope>provided</scope>
      <type>jar</type>
    </dependency>

    <dependency>
      <groupId>com.google.android</groupId>
      <artifactId>android-test</artifactId>
      <version>4.1.1.4</version>
      <scope>provided</scope>
    </dependency>
  </dependencies>
</project>
```

You may have noticed that the version of android-test library is different from the Android library version. Recall from the previous chapter Maven we manually added the `android.jar` library to our local maven repository. One might think that this could be done also for the `android-test.jar` library. The problem is that this library is not included in Android SDK, and so we need to stick to the latest available library that can be found in a public repository.

We are almost ready to write and run our first activity unit test. There is one last thing we need to modify to the module we created. Like we have already discussed, these tests require an emulator to run and so, in practice, this module is an Android application that needs a manifest file. We have to change the manifest file created by the archetype. Let's take a look how this should look like and explain the most important parts in the next section:

```xml
<?xml version="1.0" encoding="UTF-8"?>
<manifest
xmlns:android="http://schemas.android.com/apk/res/android"
  package="com.packt.androidMaven.tests"
  android:versionCode="1"
  android:versionName="1.0-SNAPSHOT" >
  <application android:allowBackup="true">
    <uses-library android:name="android.test.runner"/>
  </application>
  <instrumentation
  android:name="android.test.InstrumentationTestRunner"
  android:targetPackage="com.packt.androidMaven"
  android:label="Unit Tests of Android Maven App."/>
</manifest>
```

Running Android unit tests with Maven

It's a good practice to place our tests in a different package than the package used inside the application module. Keep in mind that our test classes should be placed under the `/src/main/java/` location and not under `/src/test/java`, because they are considered as typical code to run in a device or an emulator.

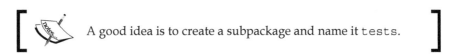 A good idea is to create a subpackage and name it `tests`.

The name of the test package should be described inside the `manifest` tag. Then, we need to specify that this module is a test project by setting the `uses-library` tag inside the `application` tag as is shown in the preceding example. Finally, we need to drive the instrumentation process by setting the responsible class, the target package (our tests should be located there), and optionally a name of this instrumentation.

Let's review the code of our Android application. It consists of two very simple activities. The first one, BookActivity, invokes a method from a business layer class and displays a text and a button. Clicking on this button, the second activity AuthorActivity is started with an intent with some custom attributes. Both classes are located under `/src/main/java/com/packt/androidMaven` package of the `AndroidTier` module:

```java
package com.packt.androidMaven;

import android.app.Activity;
import android.content.Intent;
import android.os.Bundle;
import android.view.View;
import android.view.View.OnClickListener;
import android.widget.Button;
import android.widget.TextView;
import com.packt.androidmaven.model.Book;
import com.packt.androidmaven.service.BookService;
import com.packt.androidmaven.service.BookServiceImpl;

public class BookActivity extends Activity {
  private Button button;
  private TextView textView;
  public final static String AUTHOR =
  "com.packt.androidMaven.AUTHOR";

  @Override
  public void onCreate(Bundle savedInstanceState) {
    super.onCreate(savedInstanceState);
    setContentView(R.layout.activity_main);
    setTextValue();
    addListenerOnButton();
  }

  private void setTextValue() {
    BookService bookService = new BookServiceImpl();
    final Book book = bookService.createBook("Maven and Android",
    "eBook", "black", 150);
    textView = (TextView) findViewById(R.id.text1);
    textView.setText(book.toString());
  }

  public void addListenerOnButton() {
    button = (Button) findViewById(R.id.button1);
```

```
    button.setOnClickListener(new OnClickListener() {
      @Override
      public void onClick(View view) {
        Intent intent = new Intent(view.getContext(),
        AuthorActivity.class);
        intent.putExtra(AUTHOR, "Patroklos Papapetrou");
        startActivity(intent);
      }
    });
  }
}

package com.packt.androidMaven;

import android.app.Activity;
import android.content.Intent;
import android.os.Bundle;
import android.widget.TextView;

public class AuthorActivity extends Activity {
  @Override
  public void onCreate(Bundle savedInstanceState) {
    super.onCreate(savedInstanceState);
    Intent intent = getIntent();
    String message = intent.getStringExtra(BookActivity.AUTHOR);
    TextView textView = new TextView(this);
    textView.setTextSize(40);
    textView.setText(message);
    setContentView(textView);
  }
}
```

Now, create a JUnit 3 test class and name it BookActivityTest inside the
`AndroidUnitTests` module under the `/src/main/java/com/packt/androidMaven`
directory. The reason why we are using JUnit 3 is because Android testing is built on
the top of this version and JUnit 4 is not currently supported.

 If you want to experiment with JUnit 4 testing in Android, then
you can try this open source library `https://github.com/dthommes/JUnit4Android`. Since it's not officially supported
and not fully compatible with Android testing, we will stick with
JUnit 3 and use this for the book examples.

Here's the JUnit 3 test class that will test our activity in isolation:

```
package com.packt.androidMaven.tests;

import android.content.Intent;
import android.widget.TextView;
import android.widget.Button;
import android.test.ActivityUnitTestCase;
import android.test.suitebuilder.annotation.SmallTest;
import com.packt.androidMaven.BookActivity;
import com.packt.androidMaven.R;

public class BookActivityTest extends ActivityUnitTestCase<BookActivity> {
  BookActivity bookActivity;
  private TextView textView;
  private Button button;
  public BookActivityTest() {
    super(BookActivity.class);
  }

  @Override
  protected void setUp() throws Exception {
    super.setUp();
    startActivity(new
    Intent(getInstrumentation().getTargetContext(),
    BookActivity.class), null, null);
    bookActivity = (BookActivity) getActivity();
    textView = (TextView) bookActivity.findViewById(R.id.text1);
    button = (Button) bookActivity.findViewById(R.id.button1);
  }

  @Override
  protected void tearDown() throws Exception {
    super.tearDown();
  }

  @SmallTest
  public void testPreconditions() {
    assertNotNull(button);
    assertNotNull(textView);
  }

  @SmallTest
```

```
public void testButtonLabel() {
  String actual = button.getText().toString();
  String expected = "View Author Name!";
  assertEquals(expected, actual);
}

@SmallTest
public void testTextViewText() {
  String actual = textView.getText().toString();
  String expected = "Book{id=null, title='Maven and Android',
  format='eBook', color='black', numberOfPages=150,
  brandNew=null}";
  assertEquals(expected, actual);
}
}
```

Let's quickly explain the test code, as it's not inside the scope of this book. Each test class should extend the base `android.test.ActivityUnitTestCase` class and initialize it with the activity class under test. It's a good practice to initialize the activity in the `@setUp` method. Then, we should get a reference to the started activity and references to all objects that we need to test. In our case, we got reference to the `TextView` view and the `Button` objects. Another good practice is to have a test method with the name `testPreconditions` in order to verify that the activity was initialized properly and all object references are available. Finally, we can write the actual tests. In the example class, we test the labels of the button and the text displayed. Of course, you can extend your test cases to completely test every aspect of the expected view of the target activities.

If you are not familiar with the `@SmallTest` annotation on the top of each test method, then you might want to take a look at this article: `http://googletesting.blogspot.gr/2010/12/test-sizes.html` that clearly explains their meaning. In short, we can specify three types of tests:w

- Small: This test doesn't interact with any file system or network
- Medium: This test accesses file systems on box that is running tests
- Large: This test accesses external file systems, networks, and so on

We are ready to run our activity unit test. But wait! Don't be fooled. We will not run the tests like typical unit tests. Take the following command:

```
mvn clean test
```

This command will run nothing because there are not tests, like we explained, under the `/src/test/java` package. Instead, we should open a terminal, navigate to the `AndroidUnitTests` folder, and run the following command:

```
mvn clean install
```

By default, this command will try to deploy the target application to all connected devices and running emulators; so, we advise you to connect to at least one device or run the emulator of your choice like we discussed in *Chapter 2, Starting the Development Phase* before you try to run the tests. Later on in this book, we will see how to configure testing on specific devices or emulators. The expected output of the preceding command should contain, among others, the following screenshot:

Real unit testing with Robolectric

So far, we saw how to run Android unit tests using Maven in an emulator or a real device (smart phone, tablet, and so on). If you have followed the examples provided in this chapter, you should have noticed by now that running activity unit tests is quite slow. Every time we need to follow the cycle of building the project, then deploy this to the device/emulator, and finally launch the application and run the tests. This automatically is done by Maven, but it is clearly not according to one of the core concepts of Unit testing: Run tests fast!

There must be a more clever way to do this, and it has a name from the future: Robolectric (`http://robolectric.org/`) is an Android unit testing framework that lets us run unit tests inside the **Java Virtual Machine (JVM)** of our development environment in a couple of seconds without the need of Android SDK. And it's getting even better. We can use our favorite JUnit 4 style to run our test classes, which is far better than the old JUnit 3 style, and we don't need a dedicated module to drive the execution in devices/emulators. Let's take a look right away at the steps needed to run Robolectric tests with Maven. TestNG is not supported currently, out of the box, by Robolectric.

Configuring Robolectric with Maven

Integrating Maven with Robolectric is quite simple. All we have to do is to add the following couple of dependencies in the `pom.xml` file of our `AndroidTier` module:

```xml
<dependency>
  <groupId>junit</groupId>
  <artifactId>junit</artifactId>
  <version>${junit.version}</version>
  <scope>test</scope>
</dependency>
<dependency>
  <groupId>org.robolectric</groupId>
  <artifactId>robolectric</artifactId>
  <version>${robolectric.version}</version>
  <scope>test</scope>
</dependency>
```

The versions of the dependencies can be specified as properties like this:

```xml
<properties>
  <robolectric.version>2.2</robolectric.version>
  <junit.version>4.11</junit.version>
</properties>
```

Bear in mind that since both of these dependencies are needed only for test execution, we specify the correct scope when declaring them.

Running Robolectric unit tests

Now, it's time to write a Robolectric test to verify the view of our `BookActivity` class. This test class can be perfectly placed under the `/src/test/java/com/packt/androidMaven` package of the `AndroidTier` module. You can find its implementation as follows:

```java
package com.packt.androidMaven;

import android.widget.Button;
import android.widget.TextView;
import static org.hamcrest.CoreMatchers.equalTo;
import static org.junit.Assert.assertThat;
import org.junit.Before;
import org.junit.Test;
import org.junit.runner.RunWith;
import org.robolectric.Robolectric;
```

```
import org.robolectric.RobolectricTestRunner;

@RunWith(RobolectricTestRunner.class)
public class RobolectricBookActivityTest {
  private BookActivity bookActivity;
  private TextView textView;
  private Button button;

  @Before
  public void init(){
    bookActivity =
    Robolectric.buildActivity(BookActivity.class).create().get();
    textView = (TextView) bookActivity.findViewById(R.id.text1);
    button = (Button) bookActivity.findViewById(R.id.button1);
  }

  @Test
  public void testButtonLabel() {
    String actual = button.getText().toString();
    String expected = "View Author Name!";
    assertThat(expected, equalTo(actual));
  }

  @Test
  public void testTextViewText() {
    String actual = textView.getText().toString();
    String expected = "Book{id=null, title='Maven and Android',
    format='eBook', color='black', numberOfPages=150,
    brandNew=null}";
    assertThat(expected, equalTo(actual));
  }
}
```

The idea is exactly the same with the test cases we discussed in the previous paragraphs. Before each test, we create the activity by invoking the `Robolectric.buildActivity()` method and we get a reference to the components under testing. Then, we can write test methods that assert their expected behavior and attributes. As you can see, the test is a pure JUnit 4 class, and the only line that makes this particular to the Robolectric execution is that the class is annotated to run using the `RobolectricTestRunner` attribute.

To run our test, simply open a terminal, navigate to the application folder `AndroidTier`, and run the command as shown in the following screenshot:

```
mvn clean test
```

```
T E S T S
--------------------------------------------------------------------
Running com.packt.androidMaven.RobolectricBookActivityTest
WARNING: no system properties value for ro.build.date.utc
DEBUG: Loading resources for com.packt.androidMaven from .\res...
DEBUG: Loading resources for android from jar:c:\repo\org\robolectric\android-re
s\4.1.2_r1_rc\android-res-4.1.2_r1_rc-real.jar!/res...
Tests run: 2, Failures: 0, Errors: 0, Skipped: 0, Time elapsed: 5.882 sec - in c
om.packt.androidMaven.RobolectricBookActivityTest

Results :

Tests run: 2, Failures: 0, Errors: 0, Skipped: 0

[INFO] --------------------------------------------------------------
[INFO] BUILD SUCCESS
[INFO] --------------------------------------------------------------
[INFO] Total time: 9.446 s
[INFO] Finished at: 2015-01-24T17:24:25+02:00
[INFO] Final Memory: 23M/310M
[INFO] --------------------------------------------------------------
```

The output will look similar to the following:

Test run: 2, Failures: 0, Errors: 0, Skipped: 0

 You don't need to worry about the warning as it makes no harm. Many people have the same question and there is an open ticket (https://github.com/robolectric/robolectric/issues/1251) to fix it or provide a clear solution, but for now let's ignore it as it doesn't affect the test execution.

If you want to run only a specific test class, you can simply run the following command:

```
mvn clean test -Dtest=RobolectricBookActivityTest
```

You can also use your favorite IDE to do so since all of them provide such features. You can see the results of running Robolectric unit tests inside an IDE as shown in the following screenshot:

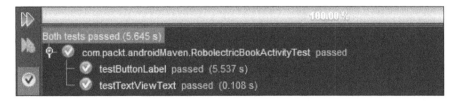

Best approach

Isn't it so cool that we don't need a different module for writing unit tests any more? Of course, it is; so you might wonder by now, which of the two approaches we discussed in this chapter is better to follow. The standard way suggested by Google or the Robolectric way? Although there is no silver bullet, we favor the latter for the reasons we mentioned in the previous section.

We need to be aware, however, that Robolectric may not support (now or in the future) components or behavior needed for completely testing an activity. Furthermore, Robolectric doesn't test activities against real devices or emulators and this might not catch corner case or incompatibilities or issues with particular versions and devices. In this case, we have two options:

- Use a combination of the two practices we discussed so far. Have Robolectric tests during the development but let a build server run the instrumentation tests. This way, we can have fast tests during development but also catch problems when the application runs on a real device.
- Leave the parts that are not supported by Robolectric to be integration tested as we will see in the next chapter.

In all cases, it's up to you to decide based on your experience and skills, your requirements and the complexity of your application. The good thing is that we have choices, and Maven is here to support our decisions and easily drive the execution of any tests.

Measuring test coverage

Having a complete test suites of the source code is very important to know that the application is bug-free and it has the expected behavior. However, when the application is growing, it's hard to keep track of which classes are adequately tested or not. It's hard to know, on other words, the test coverage of our application.

Thankfully, there are several tools that compute the test coverage, and they integrate very well with Maven; so in this section we will pick two of them (the most popular and stable ones) and we will see what is the necessary configuration to gather this information while running our unit tests.

JaCoCo

Java Code Coverage (JaCoCo) (`http://www.eclemma.org/jacoco/trunk/doc/maven.html`) tool has become the most popular tool for java code coverage in the last couple of years. The main reasons that made it the first choice is that it is free/open source, it continuously evolves, it is fast, and does on-the-fly bytecode instrumentation which leads to more accurate results of code coverage, whereas the majority of the other tools does offline instrumentation. Maven integration is supported out of the box by a very easy to configure plugin, and in this section we will briefly describe the steps to integrate it with our application.

The modifications we will make in order to use JaCoCo will be done in the parent `pom.xml` file so that all modules can use it without any additional change. We will create a Maven profile, and we will configure it to execute JaCoCo for computing coverage and creating an HTML report.

> Maven profiles are mostly used to provide customizable configuration for different environments or to provide optional tasks during a build. Explaining the details of Maven profiles is out of the context of this book; so for more details we suggest that you take a look at Maven's official page about profiles `http://maven.apache.org/guides/introduction/introduction-to-profiles.html`.

Locate the parent `pom.xml` and add the following section. Usually, the `profiles` tag is placed near the end of the file:

```
<profiles>
  <profile>
    <id>jacoco</id>
      <build>
        <plugins>
          <plugin>
            <groupId>org.jacoco</groupId>
            <artifactId>jacoco-maven-plugin</artifactId>
            <version>0.7.2.201409121644</version>
            <executions>
              <execution>
                <id>default-prepare-agent</id>
                <goals>
                  <goal>prepare-agent</goal>
                </goals>
              </execution>
              <execution>
```

```
            <id>default-report</id>
            <phase>prepare-package</phase>
            <goals>
                <goal>report</goal>
            </goals>
          </execution>
          <execution>
            <id>default-check</id>
            <goals>
                <goal>check</goal>
            </goals>
          </execution>
        </executions>
        <configuration>
          <excludes>
            <exclude>**/R.class</exclude>
            <exclude>**/R$*.class</exclude>
            <exclude>**/BuildConfig.class</exclude>
          </excludes>
        </configuration>
      </plugin>
    </plugins>
  </build>
 </profile>
</profiles>
```

In a few words, this profile defines the version of the maven-jacoco plugin and describes what actions should be done in each phase of the Maven build life cycle. Finally, we exclude some android-specific autogenerated code because we don't want to pollute the code coverage report with classes that we cannot affect.

To instruct Maven to use JaCoCo for code coverage and generate report, we need to run the following command:

```
mvn clean package -Pjacoco
```

Let's elaborate a little more about this command. The -Pjacoco command tells Maven to find the profile named jacoco and use it during its execution. This practically means that all configurations included in this profile will be added to the configuration included in the <build> tag of the pom.xml file. Additionally, we need to specify the package Maven phase because we have instructed JaCoCo to produce the report during the prepare-package Maven phase. Run the following command:

```
mvn clean test -Pjacoco
```

The coverage will be computed and stored in a binary (not human-readable) file named `jacoco.exec`, located under the target folder, but no HTML reports will be generated.

The last step is to see the coverage report. Find and open the `/target/site/jacoco/index.html` file with your favorite browser / html viewer and it will look like the following image:

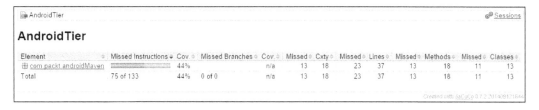

You can click on the package and see the details about the coverage of each class as shown in the following image:

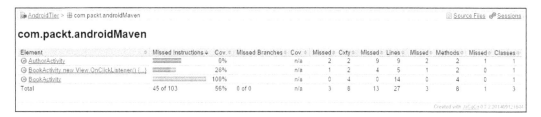

Then, you can drill down to the class level and see the coverage of each individual file as illustrated in the next image:

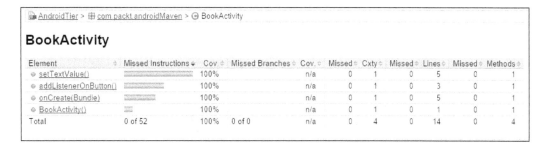

Cobertura

A very reliable alternative to JaCoCo is the **Cobertura** code coverage tool (http://mojo.codehaus.org/cobertura-maven-plugin/). We can add like we did with JaCoCo, a new profile to configure the cobertura-maven plugin as shown next. You don't need to delete the JaCoCo profile. They can live with both of them in the same pom.xml file:

```
<profile>
  <id>cobertura</id>
  <build>
    <plugins>
      <plugin>
        <groupId>org.codehaus.mojo</groupId>
        <artifactId>cobertura-maven-plugin</artifactId>
        <version>2.5.2</version>
        <configuration>
          <instrumentation>
            <excludes>
              <exclude>**/R.class</exclude>
              <exclude>**/R$*.class</exclude>
              <exclude>**/BuildConfig.class</exclude>
            </excludes>
          </instrumentation>
        </configuration>
      </plugin>
    </plugins>
  </build>
</profile>
```

As you can see, we exclude again the classes that we don't want to get reports for coverage and declare the name and version of the plugin.

 Keep in mind that although there is a newest cobertura-maven plugin (2.6), we use the previous version (2.5.2) because it's not compatible with the Robolectric testing framework and needs manual declaration of some dependencies.

Now, let's run the following Maven command to run our tests including the cobertura plugin:

```
mvn clean package cobertura:cobertura -Pcobertura
```

To see the generated HTML report by the plugin, we can just open this file
`:/target/site/cobertura/index.html` and then we can navigate from the
application level to the package level and the class level just like we did with the
JaCoCo report. The following image shows how a cobertura report looks:

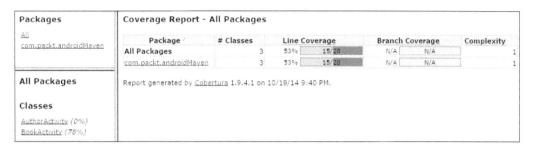

Summary

This chapter was dedicated to the Android unit testing. We covered the two different
ways of testing activities (with and without the usage of emulators/devices), and we
saw how to get reports about the code coverage. By now, you should be able to:

- Understand the difference between unit and integration testing
- Run unit tests in device/emulator using the Android testing library
- Run pure JUnit 4 tests using the Robolectric testing framework
- Configure Maven to generate code coverage reports using JaCoCo
  and Cobertura

In the next chapter, we will continue our discussion about testing. This time,
we will cover tools for integration testing that work well with maven.

4
Integration Testing

This chapter continues our discussion about Android application testing. *Chapter 3, Unit Testing* was dedicated to unit testing, but this one is about integration testing. We have categorized integration testing into instrumentation testing and **Graphical User Interface (GUI)** testing. This classification might not be very clear to you; so let us explain the reasoning behind this decision.

Both these types of testing require the presence of an emulator or a real Android device. Instrumentation testing mostly focuses on verifying the interaction between activities and intents, while GUI testing ensures that the user interface (UI) components have the expected behavior. This statement does not exclude instrumentation testing from verifying UI components or vice versa. In the following sections, we will cover two tools of each category and the corresponding Maven plugins that let us automate their execution and their reporting capabilities.

Like we already made clear, our intention is not to provide a reference for the tools we cover, although you can learn more than the basics to start using them with your application. Our goal is to give you a practical guide on how to set up your Maven configuration to effectively use these tools in your development life cycle. For the purpose of a complete and working example, we will show you some sample code in order to see these tools in action.

The first part of this chapter discusses the framework provided by Android SDK and the necessary Maven configuration you need to make it work. It also presents an alternative way of doing instrumentation testing using Spoon. The second part is dedicated to GUI testing by covering Selendroid and Robotium, two of the most popular tools in this field.

Fundamentals of instrumentation testing

Before we see how we can configure Maven to execute Android instrumentation tests, let us elaborate a little more about instrumentation testing. To run such tests, you will want to set up two things. First, you need a project that contains your tests, and second you need to deploy your application to a device or a running emulator. Then, you will be able to run the tests against the deployed application. You should be familiar with this structure, as we have already seen it in the previous chapter when we discussed unit testing as an activity.

The difference, however, is that activity unit testing is limited to testing one activity in isolation of the rest of the system, whereas instrumentation testing can verify the interaction of all Android components: activities, content providers, and services. You can start activities by other activities, make use of content providers and consume services and run complete test scenarios in various Android versions and devices.

This last statement is very critical, and it is even more important that the tool or the build framework you will choose to run your tests. Verifying your application in as many as possible target devices should be your number one priority in your integration testing strategy. Then, the tools, the configuration, and everything else comes in.

Now that we set the pace about instrumentation testing, it is time to discover what Android offers us out of the box, and how you can easily configure Maven to do it.

Running Android instrumentation tests

Android uses, like we already saw, JUnit 3. It is the underlying framework to support instrumentation testing execution. All the tests you will write need to extend one of the following classes that extend the basic class `ActivityTestCase`:

- `ActivityInstrumentationTestCase2`: This class is used for running activity tests

- `ProviderTestCase2`: This class is used for running tests of content providers and making sure that your tests always run against a clean dataset

- `ServiceTestCase`: This class is used for validating the various states of your services

 Keep in mind also that each of the previously mentioned base test classes provide specific methods and features that facilitate the testing of their target components.

Creating a dedicated integration testing module

Our first step is to create a new dedicated Maven module that will host our instrumentation test cases. You should by now be able to create a new Maven module but for clarity we include the series of required steps.

Open a terminal and navigate to the root folder of the application. Then, type the following to create a new module:

```
mvn archetype:generate \
  -DarchetypeArtifactId=android-quickstart \
  -DarchetypeGroupId=de.akquinet.android.archetypes \
  -DarchetypeVersion=1.1.0 \
  -DgroupId=com.packt.androidMaven \
  -DartifactId=AndroidIntegrationTests \
  -Dversion=1.0-SNAPSHOT \
  -Dplatform=21 \
  --batch-mode \
```

You can verify that the Maven module was correctly created by following the same steps we covered in *Chapter 3, Unit Testing* when created a similar Maven module for activity unit testing.

Double-check also that the `<modules>` tag in your parent `pom.xml` file (the `pom.xml` file found in the project's root folder) looks like the following snippet:

```
<modules>
    <module>model</module>
    <module>service</module>
    <module>AndroidTier</module>
    <module>AndroidUnitTests</module>
    <module>AndroidIntegrationTests</module>
</modules>
```

Then, you should include in the newly created `AndroidIntegrationTest` module's `pom.xml` file, like we did in the unit testing module, the dependency of the Android application that our integration tests will run against, and finally we should add a similar manifest file that describes the purpose of this module. Next, you can see how the `pom.xml` file should look. If you compare it with the file generated by the Maven archetype, you will notice that we have removed all the configurations that are already defined on the parent `pom.xml` file:

```
<?xml version="1.0" encoding="UTF-8"?>
<project xmlns="http://maven.apache.org/POM/4.0.0"
```

```
xmlns:xsi="http://www.w3.org/2001/XMLSchema-instance"
xsi:schemaLocation="http://maven.apache.org/POM/4.0.0 http://maven
.apache.org/xsd/maven -4.0.0.xsd">
  <modelVersion>4.0.0</modelVersion>
  <parent>
    <groupId>com.packt.androidMaven</groupId>
    <artifactId>sampleProject</artifactId>
    <version>1.0-SNAPSHOT</version>
  </parent>
  <artifactId>AndroidIntegrationTests</artifactId>
  <packaging>apk</packaging>
  <dependencies>
    <dependency>
      <groupId>com.packt.androidMaven</groupId>
      <artifactId>AndroidTier</artifactId>
      <version>${project.version}</version>
      <scope>provided</scope>
      <type>jar</type>
    </dependency>
    <dependency>
      <groupId>com.google.android</groupId>
      <artifactId>android-test</artifactId>
      <scope>provided</scope>
    </dependency>
  </dependencies>
</project>
```

Again, like we did in *Chapter 3, Unit Testing*, we should simplify the corresponding `AndroidManifest.xml` file created by the archetype. Here's how it should look. It's exactly the same with the file we saw in the previous chapter. We just changed the label to distinguish them:

```
<?xml version="1.0" encoding="UTF-8"?>
<manifest
xmlns:Android="http://schemas.android.com/apk/res/android"
  package="com.packt.androidMaven.tests"
  android:versionCode="1"
  android:versionName="1.0-SNAPSHOT" >
  <application android:allowBackup="true">
    <uses-library android:name="android.test.runner"/>
  </application>
  <instrumentation android:name=
  "android.test.InstrumentationTestRunner"
    android:targetPackage="com.packt.androidMaven"
    android:label="Integration Tests of Android Maven App."/>
</manifest>
```

Writing a simple instrumentation activity test

Before we give you the code of a very simple test class, let us remind you that instrumentation tests should be placed under /src/main/java/ location and not under /src/test/java location, because they are considered as typical code which is supposed to be executed in a real device or a running emulator. Keeping a consistency across all Maven modules is always a good practice; so, we suggest that all instrumentation tests are placed under the com.packt.androidMaven.tests package. This is also the package name we included in the AndroidManifest.xml file which was shown in the previous section.

Now, it is time to write a test case that validates the behavior of our little activity class BookActivity. This time, we don't need to implicitly start the activity like we did in the unit test example we saw in *Chapter 3, Unit Testing*, but the Android test framework will do this for us when we run the instrumentation test case. We don't want to also test the existence and appearance of all components. Instead, we want to verify that when the user clicks on the activity's button, then a new activity AuthorActivity is started.

Here's the code of our instrumentation test case:

```
package com.packt.androidMaven.tests;

import android.app.Instrumentation.ActivityMonitor;
import android.test.ActivityInstrumentationTestCase2;
import android.test.suitebuilder.annotation.SmallTest;
import android.widget.Button;
import com.packt.androidMaven.AuthorActivity;
import com.packt.androidMaven.BookActivity;
import com.packt.androidMaven.R;
import static junit.framework.Assert.assertNotNull;

public class BookActivityTest extends ActivityInstrumentationTestCase2
<BookActivity> {
  private BookActivity bookActivity;
  private Button button;
  public BookActivityTest() {
    super(BookActivity.class);
  }

  @Override
  protected void setUp() throws Exception {
    super.setUp();
    bookActivity = (BookActivity) getActivity();
    assertNotNull(bookActivity);
```

```
    button = (Button) bookActivity.findViewById(R.id.button1);
  }

  @Override
  protected void tearDown() throws Exception {
    super.tearDown();
  }

  @SmallTest
  public void testClickButton() {
    ActivityMonitor activityMonitor =
    getInstrumentation().
    addMonitor(AuthorActivity.class.getName(), null, false);
    bookActivity.runOnUiThread(new Runnable() {
      @Override
      public void run() {
        button.performClick();
      }
    });
    AuthorActivity authorActivity = (AuthorActivity)
    getInstrumentation().waitForMonitorWithTimeout
    (activityMonitor, 5000);
    assertNotNull(authorActivity);
    authorActivity.finish();
  }
}
```

Let's explain some parts of the code, although it's not the main purpose of this book. The meat of the test case is found in `testClickButton()` test method. First, we need to register the next activity – the one that will be opened when we click on our button – that needs to be monitored. This is done by adding an `AcitivityMonitor` parameter to the current instrumentation that monitors the `AuthorActivity` class. Then, we open the activity by performing a button-click inside a UI thread. Finally, we get a reference to the activity that is monitored by the `AcitivityMonitor` parameter, and we check to see if it is null or not. Don't forget to also close the opened activity, especially if you have some more tests in the same class.

Let's build the complete package by skipping any unit tests by running the following Maven command in the root folder of our application.

`mvn clean package -DskipTests` to run our instrumentation test – assuming that you already have a real device connected or a running emulator and that the actual Android application is already deployed – we need to execute the following Maven command from a terminal inside the `AndroidIntegrationTests` directory:

`mvn clean install`

Remember that our test code is not placed in Maven's test folder and so we can't execute the tests by the typical command such as follows:

```
mvn clean test
```

If everything goes right (it should!), you will see something like the following screenshot when the Maven command finishes:

```
[INFO] Found 1 devices connected with the Android Debug Bridge
[INFO] android.device parameter not set, using all attached devices
[INFO] Device CB5124BWNU_Sony_C5303 found.
[INFO] CB5124BWNU_Sony_C5303 :    Successfully installed C:\dev\android\packt\And
roidMavenDevelopment\Chapter4\AndroidIntegrationTests\target\AndroidIntegrationT
ests.apk to CB5124BWNU_Sony_C5303
[INFO]
[INFO] --- android-maven-plugin:3.8.2:internal-integration-test (default-interna
l-integration-test) @ AndroidIntegrationTests ---
[INFO] Found 1 devices connected with the Android Debug Bridge
[INFO] android.device parameter not set, using all attached devices
[INFO] Device CB5124BWNU_Sony_C5303 found.
[INFO] CB5124BWNU_Sony_C5303 :    Running instrumentation tests in com.packt.andr
oidMaven.tests
[INFO] CB5124BWNU_Sony_C5303 :       Run started: com.packt.androidMaven.tests, 1
tests:
[INFO] CB5124BWNU_Sony_C5303 :       Start [1/1]: com.packt.androidMaven.tests.B
ookActivityTest#testClickButton
[INFO] CB5124BWNU_Sony_C5303 :       End [1/1]: com.packt.androidMaven.tests.Boo
kActivityTest#testClickButton
[INFO] CB5124BWNU_Sony_C5303 :       Run ended: 1021 ms
[INFO]    Tests run: 1,  Failures: 0,  Errors: 0
```

If you're running instrumentation tests on a slow device or emulator, you might also notice that all interactions instructed in the tests are displayed while running the tests. This is one of the major reasons why we have classified under unit testing, tests that validate activities in isolation. This applies to, when talking about integration tests in Android.

Grabbing screenshots with Spoon

A typical Android application consists of several activities with many components and various flows of user interaction. Instrumentation tests should be able to cover if not all, most of the activity flows; so, hundreds of instrumentation tests might run every time the corresponding Maven goal is invoked. It is also very common during the development cycles that some tests might get broken due to some recent changes or new Android SDKs or new incompatible devices. Maven can report on the errors found during a test run, but in some cases the information provided is not enough. A picture worth a thousand words, so wouldn't be much better if we could have a report of all screenshots taken during integration test execution?

Spoon (`http://square.github.io/spoon/`) comes to the rescue and allows us to do two things that are not offered through the Android testing framework. First while running the tests we can grab screenshots and second, after finishing the test execution, we can produce a more human-readable test report. But there's more. Spoon can run all your instrumentation tests across all connected devices or running emulators and produce comprehensive reports per device or per test case. Let's take a look right away of the steps needed to drive instrumentation tests using Spoon with Maven.

Configuring Spoon with Maven

For clarity and to avoid mixing standard Android instrumentation tests with Spoon-driven tests, let's create a new Maven module like we previously did in this chapter, but this time we should give a different name to the module; that is, `SpoonIntegrationTests`. Here's the corresponding Maven command line to execute inside the root folder of our application:

```
mvn archetype:generate \
  -DarchetypeArtifactId=android-quickstart \
  -DarchetypeGroupId=de.akquinet.android.archetypes \
  -DarchetypeVersion=1.1.0 \
  -DgroupId=com.packt.androidMaven \
  -DartifactId=SpoonIntegrationTests \
  -Dversion=1.0-SNAPSHOT \
  -Dplatform=21 \
  --batch-mode \
```

Integrating Maven with Spoon requires a series of steps. First, we need to add a dependency to the Spoon client and the Spoon Maven plugin in the `pom.xml` file of our `SpoonIntegrationTests` module. Next you can find the `pom.xml` file of the newly created Spoon module, as it should look like this:

```xml
<?xml version="1.0" encoding="UTF-8"?>
<project xmlns="http://Maven.apache.org/POM/4.0.0"
xmlns:xsi="http://www.w3.org/2001/XMLSchema-instance"
xsi:schemaLocation="http://Maven.apache.org/POM/4.0.0
http://Maven.apache.org/xsd/Maven-4.0.0.xsd">
  <modelVersion>4.0.0</modelVersion>
  <parent>
    <groupId>com.packt.AndroidMaven</groupId>
    <artifactId>sampleProject</artifactId>
    <version>1.0-SNAPSHOT</version>
  </parent>
```

```
<artifactId>SpoonIntegrationTests</artifactId>
<packaging>apk</packaging>
<properties>
  <spoon.version>1.1.2</spoon.version>
</properties>
<dependencies>
  <dependency>
    <groupId>com.packt.androidMaven</groupId>
    <artifactId>AndroidTier</artifactId>
    <version>${project.version}</version>
    <scope>provided</scope>
    <type>jar</type>
  </dependency>
  <dependency>
    <groupId>com.packt.androidMaven</groupId>
    <artifactId>AndroidTier</artifactId>
    <version>${project.version}</version>
    <scope>provided</scope>
    <type>apk</type>
  </dependency>
  <dependency>
    <groupId>com.google.android</groupId>
    <artifactId>android-test</artifactId>
    <version>4.1.1.4</version>
    <scope>provided</scope>
  </dependency>
  <dependency>
    <groupId>com.squareup.spoon</groupId>
    <artifactId>spoon-client</artifactId>
    <version>${spoon.version}</version>
  </dependency>
</dependencies>
<build>
  <plugins>
    <plugin>
      <groupId>com.squareup.spoon</groupId>
      <artifactId>spoon-maven-plugin</artifactId>
      <version>${spoon.version}</version>
      <configuration>
        <title>Spoon 'Android Development with Maven'
        Sample</title>
        <debug>true</debug>
      </configuration>
      <executions>
```

```
      <execution>
        <phase>integration-test</phase>
        <goals>
          <goal>run</goal>
        </goals>
      </execution>
    </executions>
  </plugin>
 </plugins>
 </build>
</project>
```

As you can see, we still need the same dependencies of the target Android application and the Android test libraries. The spoon-maven plugin is also configured to run during the Maven integration test phase. Next, we need to give our target application the following permissions in order to be allowed to take screenshots during instrumentation test execution. To do this, you should add the following lines in the `AndroidManifest.xml` file of the `AndroidTier` module.

```
<uses-permission android:name=
"android.permission.DISABLE_KEYGUARD"/>
<uses-permission android:name="android.permission.WAKE_LOCK"/>
```

Please make sure that the preceding permissions are granted only for instrumentation tests and not for production applications unless it is absolutely necessary. Ideally, we should use Maven profiles to specify a test-ready profile and a production-ready profile. Since the profile concept is covered in the next chapter, we strongly advise you, as an exercise, to come back to this one, after finishing *Chapter 5*, *Android Flavors*, and try to change our approach by introducing profiles.

You should also copy the `BookActivityTest` class we created for instrumentation tests in the previous section under the same name and same package `com/packt/androidMaven/tests` location. We are going to change it a little in a few moments, but for now don't modify it. First we need to create a new instrumentation test runner which disables the keyguard and wake up the screen during execution. For simplicity you can place it in the same package with the `BookActivityTest` class. Here's the code of the test runner class. What it actually does is to first unlock the device so that the tests can input keystrokes, and then wakes up the screen for getting screenshots:

```
package com.packt.androidMaven.tests;

import android.app.Application;
import android.app.KeyguardManager;
import android.os.PowerManager;
```

```java
import android.test.InstrumentationTestRunner;

import static android.content.Context.KEYGUARD_SERVICE;
import static android.content.Context.POWER_SERVICE;
import static android.os.PowerManager.ACQUIRE_CAUSES_WAKEUP;
import static android.os.PowerManager.FULL_WAKE_LOCK;
import static android.os.PowerManager.ON_AFTER_RELEASE;

public class SpoonInstrumentationTestRunner extends
InstrumentationTestRunner {
  @Override
  public void onStart() {
    runOnMainSync(new Runnable() {
      @Override
      public void run() {
        Application app = (Application)
        getTargetContext().getApplicationContext();
        String simpleName =
        SpoonInstrumentationTestRunner.class.getSimpleName();
        ((KeyguardManager) app.getSystemService(KEYGUARD_SERVICE))
        .newKeyguardLock(simpleName).disableKeyguard();
        ((PowerManager) app.getSystemService(POWER_SERVICE))
        .newWakeLock(FULL_WAKE_LOCK | ACQUIRE_CAUSES_WAKEUP |
        ON_AFTER_RELEASE, simpleName).acquire();
      }
    });
    super.onStart();
  }
}
```

The manifest file of our newly created module should also look like the following.
Notice that we don't anymore use the Android instrumentation test runner, but the
test runner we just created before:

```xml
<?xml version="1.0" encoding="UTF-8"?>
<manifest
xmlns:android="http://schemas.android.com/apk/res/android"
  package="com.packt.androidMaven.tests"
  android:versionCode="1"
  android:versionName="1.0-SNAPSHOT" >
  <application android:allowBackup="true">
    <uses-library android:name="android.test.runner"/>
  </application>
  <instrumentation android:name=".SpoonInstrumentationTestRunner"
    android:targetPackage="com.packt.androidMaven"
    android:label="Spoon Tests of Android Maven App."/>
</manifest>
```

Now, let's go back to the `BookActivityTest` class and instruct Spoon to grab some screenshots during test execution. Add the following line:

```
Spoon.screenshot(bookActivity, "Book_Activity_started");
```

Take this as the first line of the `testClickButton()` method and the following as the last line of the same method:

```
Spoon.screenshot(authorActivity, "Author_Activity_opened");
```

Running Spoon and viewing the reports

Now, we are ready to let Spoon drive the execution of our instrumentation tests. To do so, run the following commands from a terminal inside the Maven module folder that contains the Spoon instrumentation tests `SpoonIntegrationTest`:

mvn clean:packagemvn spoon:run

The output is completely different of what we've seen so far running standard unit and integration Android tests and this is absolutely expected because now the tests are executed by a different Maven plugin. When all tests are completed, the reports have been generated and can be found under the `/target/spoon-output` directory. Open the `index.html` file with your favorite browser, and you will get a report similar to the following image:

You can click on any device or emulator and see the detailed results for the selected target or you can click on the green bar which represents the test cases run and see the results of a specific test case.

We strongly recommend you to create some more tests on your own, add statements to grab screenshots, make some tests intentionally failing, and run all of them against several emulators. The report will be really a blast!

Working with Robotium

Robotium (`https://code.google.com/p/robotium/`) is yet another framework that focuses on instrumentation testing, but it's more friendly for UI testing. Like we did in almost every tool we have discussed so far, you need to create a separate Maven module. Here's the corresponding Maven command line to execute inside the root folder of our application:

```
mvn archetype:generate \
  -DarchetypeArtifactId=android-quickstart \
  -DarchetypeGroupId=de.akquinet.android.archetypes \
  -DarchetypeVersion=1.1.0 \
  -DgroupId=com.packt.androidMaven \
  -DartifactId=RobotiumTests \
  -Dversion=1.0-SNAPSHOT \
  -Dplatform=21 \
  --batch-mode \
```

When you are done, double-check that the parent Maven configuration file, `pom.xml`, contains the new module in the `<modules>` tag. The `pom.xml` file of the newly created module, `RobotiumTests`, should contain the required dependencies for Robotium and the application under testing like we saw in the previous sections:

```
<?xml version="1.0" encoding="UTF-8"?>
<project xmlns="http://maven.apache.org/POM/4.0.0"
xmlns:xsi="http://www.w3.org/2001/XMLSchema-instance"
xsi:schemaLocation="http://maven.apache.org/POM/4.0.0
http://maven.apache.org/xsd/maven-4.0.0.xsd">
  <modelVersion>4.0.0</modelVersion>
  <parent>
    <groupId>com.packt.androidMaven</groupId>
    <artifactId>sampleProject</artifactId>
    <version>1.0-SNAPSHOT</version>
  </parent>
  <artifactId>RobotiumTests</artifactId>
```

```xml
      <packaging>apk</packaging>
      <properties>
        <robotium.version>5.2.1</robotium.version>
      </properties>
      <dependencies>
        <dependency>
          <groupId>com.packt.androidMaven</groupId>
          <artifactId>AndroidTier</artifactId>
          <version>${project.version}</version>
          <scope>provided</scope>
          <type>jar</type>
        </dependency>
        <dependency>
          <groupId>com.packt.androidMaven</groupId>
          <artifactId>AndroidTier</artifactId>
          <version>${project.version}</version>
          <scope>provided</scope>
          <type>apk</type>
        </dependency>
        <dependency>
          <groupId>com.google.android</groupId>
          <artifactId>android-test</artifactId>
          <version>4.1.1.4</version>
          <scope>provided</scope>
        </dependency>
        <dependency>
          <groupId>com.jayway.android.robotium</groupId>
          <artifactId>robotium-solo</artifactId>
          <version>${robotium.version}</version>
        </dependency>
      </dependencies>
    </project>
```

The application should also contain the same `AndroidManifest.xml` file of the `AndroidIntegrationTests` module. You can change, however, if you want the application label to include the word "Robotium". Typically, we could merge these two modules, but for better clarity we decided to handle each tool in a different module.

A Robotium test looks similar to the classic Android instrumentation test but the library contains the `Solo` class which provides several helper methods to drive the execution of the test and the assertion of the UI components. In the following text, you can find a very simple Robotium test case. It opens the `BookActivity` activity, clicks on the button, then verifies that the second activity, `AuthorActivity`, has been opened, and finally checks that the expected text exists.

Here's the exact code of what we have discussed so far:

```
package com.packt.androidMaven.tests;

import android.test.ActivityInstrumentationTestCase2;
import android.test.suitebuilder.annotation.SmallTest;
import com.packt.androidMaven.AuthorActivity;
import com.packt.androidMaven.BookActivity;
import com.robotium.solo.Solo;
import static junit.framework.Assert.assertTrue;
import static junit.framework.Assert.fail;

public class BookActivityTest extends ActivityInstrumentationTestCase2
<BookActivity> {
  private Solo solo;
  public BookActivityTest() {
    super(BookActivity.class);
  }

  @Override
  public void setUp() throws Exception {
    solo = new Solo(getInstrumentation(), getActivity());
  }

  @Override
  public void tearDown() throws Exception {
    solo.finishOpenedActivities();
  }

  @SmallTest
  public void testClickButton() throws Exception {
    solo.clickOnButton("View Author Name!");
    if ( solo.waitForActivity(AuthorActivity.class)){
      assertTrue(solo.searchText("Patroklos Papapetrou"));
    }
    else {
      fail("No author activity started!");
    }
  }
}
```

If we compare this test with the test of page 4, we will notice that both of them set up the testing environment by initializing the activity we want to test, run the test methods, and finally release all resources. The main difference is that, when using Robotium, the code is more compact and clearly more simple and readable.

To run our test, we need to execute the following Maven command from a terminal inside the Robotium tests Maven module folder:

```
mvn clean install
```

> Please make sure that the emulator/device screen you will use to run Robotium tests is unlocked; otherwise, you will receive an error during execution. If you haven't compiled the parent project so far, you can run the following Maven command on the root folder:
>
> ```
> mvn clean package
> ```

The output is expected to be the same with the one we saw when running instrumentation tests using Android's testing framework.

UI Tests made easy with Selendroid

So far, we examined frameworks and tools that focus on Android components such as activities, services, intents, and so on. This is, with no doubt, very useful, but one of the key factors for a successful mobile application is a bug-free UI. In this section, we will discuss one of the most popular—and easy to use with Maven—tools for UI: **Selendroid** (http://selendroid.io/). One might argue that Selendroid is not the only available options for Android UI Testing, and this is absolutely true. It is a highly emerging field, but at the time of writing the book we had to pick only one of them due to the limited number of pages. We made our choice based on the level of integration with Maven, the maturity, stability, and the easiness of writing test cases.

Selendroid is a testing framework for native, hybrid, and mobile web applications based on **Selenium**, the most popular web UI testing framework. To use Selendroid, you should have a basic knowledge of Selenium because the tests are written using the Selenium 2 Client API. You can run Selendroid tests against emulators or real devices connected to the machine that runs the Selenium Client. In the remaining part of this section, we will show you how to configure Maven, then we will explore a basic Selendroid test case for our application, and finally we will see how to run the test using Maven.

Configuring Selendroid

Again, you will need to create a new Maven module and give it the following name: `SelendroidTests` with the following Maven command:

```
mvn archetype:generate \
    -DarchetypeArtifactId=android-quickstart \
    -DarchetypeGroupId=de.akquinet.android.archetypes \
```

```
-DarchetypeVersion=1.1.0 \
-DgroupId=com.packt.androidMaven \
-DartifactId=SelendroidTests \
-Dversion=1.0-SNAPSHOT \
-Dplatform=21 \
--batch-mode \
```

When you finish creating the new module, the parent Maven configuration file, pom.xml, should contain the new module in the <modules> tag, The pom.xml file of the created module should contain the required dependencies for Selendroid (the standalone server and the client) and JUnit 4, which is used as the underlying framework to run the tests. You can see how this should look:

```xml
<?xml version="1.0" encoding="UTF-8"?>
<project xmlns="http://maven.apache.org/POM/4.0.0"
xmlns:xsi="http://www.w3.org/2001/XMLSchema-instance"
xsi:schemaLocation="http://maven.apache.org/POM/4.0.0
http://maven.apache.org/xsd/maven-4.0.0.xsd">
   <modelVersion>4.0.0</modelVersion>
   <parent>
     <groupId>com.packt.androidMaven</groupId>
     <artifactId>sampleProject</artifactId>
     <version>1.0-SNAPSHOT</version>
   </parent>
   <artifactId>SelendroidTests</artifactId>
   <properties>
     <selendroid.version>0.12.0</selendroid.version>
   </properties>
   <dependencies>
     <dependency>
        <groupId>junit</groupId>
        <artifactId>junit</artifactId>
        <version>4.10</version>
     </dependency>
     <dependency>
        <groupId>io.selendroid</groupId>
        <version>${selendroid.version}</version>
        <artifactId>selendroid-standalone</artifactId>
     </dependency>
     <dependency>
        <groupId>io.selendroid</groupId>
        <version>${selendroid.version}</version>
        <artifactId>selendroid-client</artifactId>
```

```
        </dependency>
      </dependencies>
    </project>
```

Now here comes the tricky part. So far, we learned that for almost all frameworks we covered, we need to include the APK and JAR files of our target application as dependencies to the pom.xml file. For Selendroid test cases, this is not required, but it is expected that the APK file of the application to test is available in the same project. A good practice is to place it under the src/main/resources folder. This way, we can instruct Selendroid as we will see in a moment to use this APK for running the tests. Clearly, we want this step to be an automated task; so, we need to add the following section in the pom.xml file of the SelendroidTests module:

```
<build>
  <plugins>
    <plugin>
      <groupId>org.apache.maven.plugins</groupId>
      <artifactId>maven-dependency-plugin</artifactId>
      <version>2.9</version>
      <executions>
        <execution>
          <id>copy-app</id>
          <phase>generate-resources</phase>
          <goals>
            <goal>copy</goal>
          </goals>
          <configuration>
            <artifactItems>
              <artifactItem>
                <groupId>com.packt.androidMaven</groupId>
                <artifactId>AndroidTier</artifactId>
                <version>${project.version}</version>
                <type>apk</type>
                <outputDirectory>${project.build.directory}
                </outputDirectory>
                <destFileName>AndroidTier.apk</destFileName>
              </artifactItem>
            </artifactItems>
          </configuration>
        </execution>
      </executions>
    </plugin>
  </plugins>
</build>
```

The preceding configuration tells Maven to grab the `AndroidTier.apk` file, which is generated and located under the `AndroidTier/target` folder, and copy it to `src/main/resources` folder of the `SelendroidTests` module. There's one more thing we need to take care. Selendroid starts a web server on the device/emulator where the **Application Under Test (AUT)** is deployed and tested. As you already know, to allow an Android application to open network sockets we need to add the Internet permission in the `AndroidManifest.xml` file of the `AndroidTier` module:

```
<uses-permission android:name="android.permission.INTERNET"/>
```

The last step is to run the following Maven command from the root folder of the Maven project to copy the `AndroidTier.apk` file to the desired location. We don't want to run all the tests we created so far; so, it's a good idea to use the `skipTests` Maven argument:

```
mvn clean package -DskipTests
```

Now, we are ready to write a simple Selendroid test, which is discussed in the following section.

Writing Selendroid UI Tests for Maven native applications

As we already mentioned, Selendroid tests use JUnit 4; so we should place them under the `src/test/java` folder. Here's the code for a simple Selendroid test case that verifies that the label of our button:

```
package com.packt.androidMaven.tests;

import io.selendroid.SelendroidCapabilities;
import io.selendroid.SelendroidConfiguration;
import io.selendroid.SelendroidDriver;
import io.selendroid.SelendroidLauncher;

import org.junit.AfterClass;
import org.junit.Assert;
import org.junit.BeforeClass;
import org.junit.Test;
import org.openqa.selenium.By;
import org.openqa.selenium.WebDriver;
import org.openqa.selenium.WebElement;

public class SelendroidTest {
  private static SelendroidLauncher selendroidServer = null;
```

```java
    private static WebDriver driver = null;

    @BeforeClass
    public static void startSelendroidServer() throws Exception {
        if (selendroidServer != null) {
            selendroidServer.stopSelendroid();
        }
        SelendroidConfiguration config = new
        SelendroidConfiguration();
        config.addSupportedApp("target/AndroidTier.apk");
        config.setForceReinstall(true);
        selendroidServer = new SelendroidLauncher(config);
        selendroidServer.launchSelendroid();
        SelendroidCapabilities caps = new SelendroidCapabilities
        ("com.packt.AndroidMaven:1.0-SNAPSHOT");
        driver = new SelendroidDriver(caps);
    }

    @AfterClass
    public static void stopSelendroidServer() {
        if (driver != null) {
            driver.quit();
        }
        if (selendroidServer != null) {
            selendroidServer.stopSelendroid();
        }
    }

    @Test
    public void testShouldBeAbleToEnterText() {
        WebElement button = driver.findElement(By.id("button1"));
        Assert.assertNotNull(button);
        Assert.assertEquals("View Author Name!", button.getText());
    }
}
```

The code speaks for itself, but we would like to point out a couple of important things you should have in mind. The `@BeforeClass` method is responsible for starting the Selenium server using a configuration object, pointing to the APK file of the AUT. The last line of this method initializes the Selendroid driver that will run the tests of the class. It is strongly recommended, also, to use the `setForceReinstall()` method so that even if the AUT is already deployed, Selendroid will deploy the latest available version. The `@AfterClass` method stops the Selendroid driver and the Selendroid Server, which is a best practice that cleans up the resources used.

To run the tests, you can simply run the following Maven command from a terminal window in the `SelendroidTest` module. Make sure that at least one device/ emulator is connected/running to your environment:

`mvn test`

 Selendroid tests, like Robotium tests, will not run on a device/emulator that has a locked screen; so, make sure that before you run your tests you have disabled any screen locks.

The output of the preceding Maven command is usually big, and so there's no reason to display it here. You can see information messages about shell commands executed by Selendroid, starting and stopping servers on your device/emulator and executing tests. It's a good idea, however, to tell you what is going behind the scenes. The APK of the AUT is resigned again with the same certificate that the Selendroid server is signed, and both of them are deployed on the device. Then, the Selendroid client joins the game and runs the test methods. Since they are typical JUnit 4 tests, the surefire plugin will execute them and you will get the same output results like the unit tests we discussed in the previous chapter.

Other integration testing tools

There are a couple of tools that we think deserve their own little space in this integration testing chapter. We won't cover them in detail, but we want to give you some basic idea of how you can use them in a Maven environment. The reason that we didn't cover them in separate sections is that they don't have a straightforward Maven integration, and many things should be done manually:

- **Espresso** (`https://code.google.com/p/android-test-kit/wiki/ Espresso`): It is a funny-tiny framework that allows you to quickly run integration tests without worrying about waits, syncs, sleeps, and all these annoying things. The required library does not exist in any public Maven repository; so, you need to download and build the code by yourself and then add it to your local Maven repository. Then you can add the dependency to your project. The idea is again the same. You need to add the APK and JAR dependencies of the AUT in your `pom.xml` file and write instrumentation tests using Espresso's testing utilities. To run the tests, an `mvn clean install` command should be enough.

- **Appium** (http://appium.io): It is mostly known for testing iOS native applications and mobile-web applications, but it can also be used for running Android tests as well. For this purpose, you can use the java wrapper and add it as a dependency to your pom.xml file:

```
<dependency>
  <groupId>io.appium</groupId>
  <artifactId>java-client</artifactId>
  <version>2.1.0</version>
</dependency>
```

- Appium uses Selenium client; so, like Selendroid that we previously discussed, we don't need the dependencies of the AUT in the pom.xml file. However, you can't directly run the Appium server from Maven, and so it should run prior to the test execution.

- Both tools look promising, but since they don't provide an easy integration with Maven, we decided not to explain them in details. This, however, doesn't stop you from playing with them and try to develop a way to make them part of a Maven development process. Consider this as the next step of your Maven expertise you will get from this book.

Summary

This chapter was dedicated to the Android integration and UI testing. We covered four alternatives in detail to write your tests. We started by discussing the standard way of writing instrumentation tests, as proposed by the Android framework. Then, we saw some great tools like Spoon, Robotium, and Selendroid that either provide better ways to write functional tests or add more features like screensshots and better reporting. By now, you should be able to:

- Set up all tools in Maven as we discussed in this chapter
- Select the tool that fits better for your application or for your development environment
- Write the basic integration tests and run them using Maven commands

We leave behind the topics of Android testing and we can move on to the next chapter that is dedicated to how to use Maven for multi-versioned applications.

5
Android Flavors

One of the problems that many Android developers have to deal with, regardless of the build tool they are using, is the ability to create different versions of their application based on the same code base with slightly different settings, set of features, and so on. In this chapter, we discuss how we can configure Maven to automate the process of creating different application versions. In particular, we cover the following:

- Introduction to Maven profiles
- Creating profiles with different package inclusions
- Dynamically modifying project's package in manifest file
- Managing Android libraries with Maven

Problem statement

Let's face the truth. Very few developers and no companies want to write code without getting paid. Android application is not an exception to this rule. On the other hand, we can find thousands of applications available in the market place, free to download. How companies earn money while they make their applications available without a download fee? There are three popular ways to monetize a mobile application—not Android-specific:

- Support ads in the application
- Provide a minimum set of features in a free application (maybe called demo version) and the complete feature set in a paid application
- Support in-app purchases (Freemium mode)

It seems that the last one has become the number one choice, especially when we talk about applications that have to do with gaming or fun in general. But you can find thousands of nongaming-related applications in the Android Market/ Google Play that follows the first two approaches. So far so good. The problems begin when dealing with the fact that the Android Market/Google Play enforces developers to use a unique package name for each application deployed in the market place. The version concept is related to subsequent releases of the same application; so, you cannot define flavors (free, ads-supported, paid) of the same application keeping the package name untouched.

One might think that we can just change the package name inside the `AndroidManifest.xml` file, set a demo flag to `True` or `False`, depending on the version we want to build, recompile the project with the new package name, and deploy it to Android Market. This would be an ideal scenario, but unfortunately it is not that easy as it sounds.

Like we said, the application package name is configured inside the `AndroidManifest.xml` file, as you can see in the following code sample. This name will be used when uploading the application to Android Market. We will discuss about deploying applications in the next chapter:

```xml
<?xml version="1.0" encoding="utf-8"?>
<manifest xmlns:android="http://schemas.android.com/apk/res/android"
  package="com.packt.androidMaven"
  android:versionCode="1"
  android:versionName="1.0-SNAPSHOT" >
  <uses-sdk
    android:minSdkVersion="8"
    android:targetSdkVersion="21" />
  <activity android:name=".AuthorActivity" >
  </activity>
</application>
</manifest>
```

Now, try to change the value of the package name of the `AndroidTier` module `AndroidManifest.xml` file to something else ,that is, `com.packt.anroidMavenPaid`, and recompile your project. You will get some errors that look like the following:

```
COMPILATION ERROR :
-------------------------------------------------------------
com/packt/androidMaven/BookActivity.java:[23,25] package R does not exist
com/packt/androidMaven/BookActivity.java:[32,45] package R does not exist
com/packt/androidMaven/BookActivity.java:[37,41] package R does not exist
3 errors
```

This happens because when Android generates the R.java class, it uses the new package name defined in AndroidManifest.xml file. However, the imports in our Maven project across all Java classes still reference the previous name, com.packt.anroidMaven. This is our primary road block, because every time you need to release a new version you should go and manually change all imports in the application. Clearly, you never want to do this.

A possible solution would be to have two branches of the same application. One for developing the full paid version on the main branch and another one for packaging the demo/ads-supported version. This second branch should have all the required adjustments in the code to build the demo version including demo flags, different manifest file, updated imports point to another R.java class, and so on. You can try it if you want, but after some time you will find yourself doing dangerous and error-prone merges of these branches to keep them synced when you add code that should exist in both versions.

There must be a more intelligent, more automated, and developer friendly solution to overcome this problem. This solution has a name: Maven build profiles. In the next section, we will shortly discuss the basic concept of Maven profiles and then we will start configuring our application for building a demo version and a paid version.

Introducing Maven profiles

So far, our Maven configuration files, pom.xml, are quite straightforward with no advanced settings. Actually, we have already used Maven profiles in *Chapter 3*, *Unit Testing*, when we wanted to compute the code coverage of our unit tests using JaCoCo. Our case was to have this coverage computation executed only when we explicitly instruct Maven to do it.

In general, build profiles are used in several cases. The most common scenario is to make builds environment agnostic so that they can be executed in any platform or operating system without changing them every time. Profiles can also be used when we want to describe a specific set of build steps that are not required to be included in our daily builds, like the code coverage computation we discussed in *Chapter 3*, *Unit Testing*. Profiles are also used to make pom.xml files more readable. Instead of having all build steps inside the <build> tag, we can modularize them in concrete profiles that are activated by default when we trigger a build.

We can specify a profile by using a subset of the available elements we can use in the pom.xml file. When a Maven build is triggered with one or more profiles, this practically changes the pom.xml file during build time by merging the configuration provided in these profiles with the parameters used in the main configuration path.

Profiles can be defined in three levels:

- **Project level**: This defines profiles in the `pom.xml` file itself. Such profiles will be available only in the current project and also in projects that inherit from it.

- **User level**: This defines profiles in the user `settings.xml` file. This file is usually located under this folder: `%USER_HOME%/.m2/settings.xml`. Such profiles will be available for all projects of the login user.

- **Global level**: This defines profiles in the global—Maven installation `settings.xml` file. This file is usually located under this folder: `%M2_HOME%/conf/settings.xml`. Such profiles will be available for all projects run in the target machine.

 If both user level and global level settings files exist, their contents get merged, with the user-specific configuration being dominant.

Activation of build profiles can be done also in various ways including OS settings, Maven settings, based on environment variables. In our case, however, we want to trigger a profile explicitly and so we will use the command line activation like we already did in *Chapter 3, Unit Testing*. The following command describes the manual activation of profiles when running a Maven command:

```
mvn groupId:artifactId:goal -P profile-1,profile-2
```

`profile-1` and `profile-2` are profile names defined in any of the configuration levels we mentioned previously.

Creating build profiles

When developing applications that can be distributed/downloaded from Android Market/Google Play place in more than one flavor, we usually implement the project structure in such a way so that the code is needed only for a particular version that is located inside a package or a module and is completely isolated from the rest of the application. Let's focus on the user story *As a developer, I want to maintain in parallel two versions of my application, one feature-limited and a full paid version*. We can achieve this isolation by keeping the code needed for the paid version in a different package or in a completely different library. In the following section, we will show you how you can configure Maven to handle both cases and create two different build strategies. If you understand the fundamental concepts and the way we handle in Maven different versions of the same application, then you expand this knowledge to cover more than two versions, for instance, have an ads-supported version.

Separation by packaging

Let's try the first solution, Separate features by package. To demonstrate it, we will need to add a new Android activity in our `AndroidTier` Maven module, located in a different package than the one we used for the activities shown in the previous chapters. Then, we will need to modify one of our existing activities, `BookActivity.java`, and add a new button that starts the new activity only if it exists. Finally, we will create two build profiles, one that includes the new activity and one that does not.

First we create a new package named `com.packt.paid`, and add the new activity as shown here:

```
package com.packt.paid;

import android.app.Activity;
import android.os.Bundle;
import android.widget.TextView;

public class PaidActivity extends Activity {
  @Override
  public void onCreate(Bundle savedInstanceState) {
    super.onCreate(savedInstanceState);
    TextView textView = new TextView(this);
    textView.setTextSize(40);
    textView.setText("Thank you for purchasing my app!");
    setContentView(textView);
  }
}
```

Now we want to register this activity in our `AndroidManifest.xml` file but we want to allow our application to start the activity without directly calling its class name. This is needed because in the case of the free version our application will be built without the `paid` package. To do so, we need to add an intent filter in its declaration. Here is the code snippet you need to add in the `AndroidManifest.xml` file.

```
<activity android:name="com.packt.paid.PaidActivity" >
  <intent-filter>
    <action android:name="com.packt.paid.intent.action.Launch" />
    <category android:name="android.intent.category.DEFAULT" />
  </intent-filter>
</activity>
```

Finally, let's modify `BookActivity.java` class by adding a new button that, when clicked, will try to start this new activity. If it is not found, it will display a message prompting the user to purchase the paid version of the application. First, we need to register this button in the `activity_main.xml` file located under `/res/layout` folder by adding the following XML configuration:

```
<Button
  android:id="@+id/paidbutton"
  android:layout_width="wrap_content"
  android:layout_height="wrap_content"
  android:text="@string/try_me"
  android:layout_marginTop="65dp"
  android:layout_below="@+id/button1"
  android:layout_centerHorizontal="true" />
```

Don't forget to also add the new string resource we just used, `@string/try_me`, by adding the following line inside the resources tag of the `strings.xml` file located under `/res/values` folder:

```
<string name="try_me">Try me!</string>
```

Finally, here's the updated version of the `BookActivity.java` class which contains a new method to create a listener on the new button. When user clicks on this button, then our application will try to start the `PaidActivity.java` class by using the intent filter we just specified in the `AndroidManifest.xml` file. The changes from the previous version of the file are highlighted to better understand what is new in the current implementation:

```
package com.packt.androidMaven;

import android.app.Activity;
import android.content.ActivityNotFoundException;
import android.content.Intent;
import android.os.Bundle;
import android.view.View;
import android.view.View.OnClickListener;
import android.widget.Button;
import android.widget.TextView;
import android.widget.Toast;
import static android.widget.Toast.LENGTH_SHORT;
import com.packt.androidmaven.model.Book;
import com.packt.androidmaven.service.BookService;
import com.packt.androidmaven.service.BookServiceImpl;

public class BookActivity extends Activity {
```

```
private Button button;
private TextView textView;
public final static String AUTHOR = "com.packt.androidMaven.AUTHOR";

@Override
public void onCreate(Bundle savedInstanceState) {
  super.onCreate(savedInstanceState);
  setContentView(R.layout.activity_main);
  setTextValue();
  addListenerOnButton();
  addListenerOnPaidButton();
}

private void setTextValue() {
  BookService bookService = new BookServiceImpl();
  final Book book = bookService.createBook("Maven and Android",
  "eBook",
  "black", 150);
  textView = (TextView) findViewById(R.id.text1);
  textView.setText(book.toString());
}

public void addListenerOnButton() {
  button = (Button) findViewById(R.id.button1);
  button.setOnClickListener(new OnClickListener() {
    @Override
    public void onClick(View view) {
      Intent intent = new Intent(view.getContext(), AuthorActivity.
      class);
      intent.putExtra(AUTHOR, "Patroklos Papapetrou");
      startActivity(intent);
    }
  });
}

public void addListenerOnPaidButton() {
  button = (Button) findViewById(R.id.paidbutton);
  button.setOnClickListener(new OnClickListener() {
    @Override
    public void onClick(View view) {
      Intent intent = new Intent("com.packt.paid.intent.action.
      Launch");
      try {
        startActivity(intent);
      }
```

```
      catch (ActivityNotFoundException e) {
        Toast.makeText(view.getContext(), "You need to purchase the
        full version!", LENGTH_SHORT).show();
      }
    }
  });
  }
}
```

Now let's build our application by running the following Maven command in the parent folder:

```
mvn clean package -DskipTests
```

Then, we can deploy it by running the following command inside the `AndroidTier` module:

```
mvn android:deploy
```

If we run the application, we will see the main screen that now contains the new button labeled **Try me!**. If we click on it, the new activity is started and we see the message: **Thank you for purchasing my app**. The following image illustrates the expected behavior/flow of our application so far;

Now, it's time to add a new Maven profile that will build our application by excluding the `com.packt.paid` package so that when users install it they won't be able to access the `PaidActivity` class.

To do this, simply add the following XML configuration inside the `<project>` tag of AndroidTier's `pom.xml` file:

```
<profiles>
  <profile>
    <id>freeVersion</id>
```

```
<build>
  <plugins>
    <plugin>
      <groupId>org.apache.maven.plugins</groupId>
      <artifactId>maven-compiler-plugin</artifactId>
      <configuration>
        <excludes>
          <exclude>**/com/packt/paid/*.java</exclude>
        </excludes>
      </configuration>
    </plugin>
  </plugins>
</build>
</profile>
</profiles>
```

The profile we just created, when triggered, will exclude from the `.apk` file the classes that belong to the `com.packt.paid` package. To test how our application will behave with the new profile, open a terminal and execute the following command:

mvn clean package android:deploy -PfreeVersion

 If the application is already deployed to the target device/emulator, you can replace the android:deploy part with android:redeploy.

Run the application and click on the **Try me!** button. You would expect to see the message **You need to purchase the full version!**, but instead of this, the application crashes and terminates abnormally. If you debug it, you will also see that a `ClassNotFoundException` exception is thrown instead of `ActivityNotFoundException` exception, which is the expected exception that we catch inside our code. Let's see what is going on behind the scenes. The activity is registered in our `AndroidManifest.xml` file; so, Android cannot throw an `ActivityNotFoundException` exception. The device tries to start the activity but the class has been excluded from our `.apk` file, and so we get this `ClassNotFoundException` exception.

We made some progress—users cannot access the feature that is available only in the paid version—but the overall user experience is not the desired one. The problem here is that we need to remove the activity from the `AndroidManifest.xml` file. The solution is not to remove it dynamically, but instruct Maven to use another file when running the 'free version' profile. This can be done by adding some more configuration inside the `<plugins>` tag of our created profile in the AndroidTier's module `pom.xml` file. Our profile should look like the following:

```xml
<profiles>
  <profile>
    <id>freeVersion</id>
    <build>
      <plugins>
        <plugin>
          <groupId>org.apache.maven.plugins</groupId>
          <artifactId>maven-compiler-plugin</artifactId>
          <configuration>
            <excludes>
              <exclude>**/com/packt/paid/*.java</exclude>
            </excludes>
          </configuration>
        </plugin>
        <plugin>
          <groupId>com.jayway.maven.plugins.android.generation2
          </groupId>
          <artifactId>android-maven-plugin</artifactId>
          <configuration>
            <androidManifestFile>${basedir}/free/AndroidManifest.xml
            </androidManifestFile>
          </configuration>
        </plugin>
      </plugins>
    </build>
  </profile>
</profiles>
```

The added configuration instructs Maven to use the manifest file which is located under the `/free` directory. The content of this file should be the same with the original file without the code we previously added in page 4 of this chapter.

If you try to build and deploy the application using the free profile, you should notice the expected behavior: a toast message prompting the user to purchase the paid version of the applications.

Now, we can build both our free and paid versions of our application without doing any manual modification in our configuration files by just invoking different Maven commands inside the `AndroidTier` module directory, as summarized here:

- Build the complete paid version by running:

  ```
  mvn clean package
  ```

- Build the free version by running:

  ```
  mvn clean package -PfreeVersion
  ```

However, there is one thing still missing. Both versions are built using the same package name; so, based on the problem statement in the beginning of the chapter we won't be able to deploy them in Android Market/Google Play because the second one will be considered as an 'upgrade' of the first one. You can simply verify this by trying to deploy both applications in the same device/emulator using this Maven command:

```
mvn android:deploy
```

No matter what you do, the device will always have only one application installed. The one you deployed last. Let's try to fix it. We need to find a way to dynamically change the package name of the `.apk` file during our build execution without modifying the actual manifest file, because this will make our activities not to run. Our goal is to have the following package names:

- `com.packt.androidMaven.paid` package for the paid version
- `com.packt.androidMaven.free` package for the free version

First, we need to introduce a property in the `pom.xml` file of the `AndroidTier` module, which will differentiate the package name. If you see the two names more carefully, you will notice that only the last part of the package name changes; so our property should just keep this value. Enter the following line inside the `<properties>` tag:

```
<flavor>paid</flavor>
```

What we just did is to introduce a Maven property named `flavor` that has the value of `paid`. Then, we need to instruct Maven to use this property and rename the application package when creating the `.apk` file. To do so, add the following lines in the `pom.xml` file of the AndroidTier's module:

```
<build>
  <plugins>
    <plugin>
      <groupId>com.jayway.maven.plugins.android.generation2
      </groupId>
```

```
        <artifactId>android-maven-plugin</artifactId>
        <configuration>
          <renameManifestPackage>com.packt.androidMaven.${flavor}
          </renameManifestPackage>
        </configuration>
      </plugin>
    </plugins>
  </build>
```

This is done by configuring, as shown in the preceding module, the android-maven-plugin to rename the manifest package to: com.packt.androidMaven.${flavor}, where the ${flavor} variable will be replaced by its value, paid. If you build the project again, the generated .apk file will include an AndroidManifest.xml file with the expected package name which is: com.packt.androidMaven.paid. The last step to complete our configuration is to set the same property to our free profile we have previously added to the AndroidTier module's pom.xml file. This is done in order to achieve the same behavior when the profile is used. Just add the following lines inside the <profile> tag of the "free" profile:

```
<properties>
  <flavor>free</flavor>
</properties>
```

Build the project by triggering the profile for the free version:

mvn clean package -PfreeVersion

The generated .apk file will include again an AndroidManifest.xml file, but the package name now will be: com.packt.androidMaven.free.

To ensure that everything works as expected, build the free version, deploy it in a device or emulator, and run it. Verify that you don't have access to the paid feature. Then, build the full version, deploy it to the same device or emulator. You should notice that after deploying both applications, you can see two icons appearing in the target device/emulator, which is exactly our goal. The only problem now is that they both have the same name/description because both our builds use the same resource files. To overcome this last issue, we can introduce a new property, let's call it android.res.dir that will point to the resources directory of each version. We finally need to add the following line:

```
<resourceDirectory>${android.res.dir}</}</resourceDirectory>
```

This line is added inside the <configuration> tag of the android-maven-plugin just like we did with the <androidManifestFile> tag.

We leave this part as an exercise for you, create a directory /free/res, add the required resources files, and so on, and set the correct property values in the pom. xml file to validate that you have understood the concept of profiles and how you can customize the build process based on the needs of each version.

You can find the complete code of the preceding example in the GitHub repository https://github.com/ppapapetrou76/AndroidMavenDevelopment/tree/master/ Chapter5

After all these steps, we have managed to reach our goal: Parameterize our build scripts to support in-parallel versions of the same application. In the next section, we will discuss a different way to achieve the same without using Maven profiles.

Separation by library

The second approach to solve the problem of multiple versions is based on a multimodule Maven project and the concept of Android library projects.

These projects contain shareable Android source code and resources that you can reference in Android projects. This is useful when you have common code that you want to reuse. Library projects cannot be installed onto a device; however, they are pulled into the .apk file at build time.

Android-maven project files documentation: https://developer. android.com/tools/projects/index.html

In the next sections, we will guide you step by step to create such a project. The completed source code can be found in the following GitHub repository: https://github.com/ppapapetrou76/AndroidMavenDevelopment/tree/ master/Chapter5Lib

Our first step is to create a Maven multimodule project. You should be very familiar with this process—we described several times in the previous chapters, how to create a multimodule and submodules maven projects; so go on and create a parent project with three submodules named: CommonLibrary, FreeVersion and PaidVersion accordingly.

When you finish, make sure that the parent pom.xml file looks like the following file:

```xml
<?xml version="1.0" encoding="UTF-8"?>
<project xmlns="http://maven.apache.org/POM/4.0.0"
xmlns:xsi="http://www.w3.org/2001/XMLSchema-instance"
xsi:schemaLocation="http://maven.apache.org/POM/4.0.0
http://maven.apache.org/maven-v4_0_0.xsd">
```

```xml
<modelVersion>4.0.0</modelVersion>
<groupId>com.packt.androidMaven</groupId>
<artifactId>chapter5</artifactId>
<version>1.0-SNAPSHOT</version>
<packaging>pom</packaging>
<name>Chapter 5 - Library</name>
<description>Android App Development with Maven</description>

<modules>
  <module>CommonLibrary</module>
  <module>FreeVersion</module>
  <module>PaidVersion</module>
</modules>
<properties>
  <project.build.sourceEncoding>
  UTF-8</project.build.sourceEncoding>
  <platform.version>5.0.1_r2</platform.version>
  <android.plugin.version>3.8.2</android.plugin.version>
  <maven.compiler.source>1.7</maven.compiler.source>
  <maven.compiler.target>1.7</maven.compiler.target>
</properties>
<dependencyManagement>
  <dependencies>
    <dependency>
      <groupId>com.google.android</groupId>
      <artifactId>android</artifactId>
      <version>${platform.version}</version>
    </dependency>
    <dependency>
      <groupId>com.google.android</groupId>
      <artifactId>android-test</artifactId>
      <version>4.1.1.4</version>
    </dependency>
  </dependencies>
</dependencyManagement>

<build>
  <finalName>${project.artifactId}</finalName>
  <pluginManagement>
    <plugins>
      <plugin>
        <groupId>com.jayway.maven.plugins.android.generation2
        </groupId>
```

```xml
        <artifactId>android-maven-plugin</artifactId>
        <version>${android.plugin.version}</version>
        <configuration>
          <undeployBeforeDeploy>true</undeployBeforeDeploy>
        </configuration>
        <extensions>true</extensions>
      </plugin>
    </plugins>
  </pluginManagement>
  <plugins>
    <plugin>
      <groupId>com.jayway.maven.plugins.android.generation2
      </groupId>
      <artifactId>android-maven-plugin</artifactId>
      <extensions>true</extensions>
      <configuration>
        <sdk>
          <platform>21</platform>
        </sdk>
      </configuration>
    </plugin>
  </plugins>
</build>
</project>
```

The `pom.xml` file of the `CommonLibrary` module should look like the following file:

```xml
<?xml version="1.0" encoding="UTF-8"?>
<project xmlns="http://maven.apache.org/POM/4.0.0"
xmlns:xsi="http://www.w3.org/2001/XMLSchema-instance"
xsi:schemaLocation="http://maven.apache.org/POM/4.0.0
http://maven.apache.org/xsd/maven-4.0.0.xsd">
  <modelVersion>4.0.0</modelVersion>
  <parent>
    <groupId>com.packt.androidMaven</groupId>
    <artifactId>chapter5</artifactId>
    <version>1.0-SNAPSHOT</version>
  </parent>
  <artifactId>CommonLibrary</artifactId>
  <packaging>aar</packaging>

  <dependencies>
    <dependency>
      <groupId>com.google.android</groupId>
```

```
      <artifactId>android</artifactId>
      <scope>provided</scope>
    </dependency>
  </dependencies>
</project>
```

> The packaging type of this module is .AAR, which is the binary
> distribution of an Android library project. The file extension of the
> produced artifact, when building the project, should be AAR as
> well, but you can simply open the file by a zip viewer and view
> its contents that include among others the AndroidManifest.
> xml file, a classes.jar file that includes all classes of the Maven
> module, and a res folder that includes all the required resources
> for the commonly used Android components.

The pom.xml files of the other two modules should look almost identical. The only difference should be the <artifactId> tag and optionally the name of the module. You can see the Maven configuration file for the free version module as follows:

```xml
<?xml version="1.0" encoding="UTF-8"?>
<project xmlns="http://maven.apache.org/POM/4.0.0"
xmlns:xsi="http://www.w3.org/2001/XMLSchema-instance"
xsi:schemaLocation="http://maven.apache.org/POM/4.0.0
http://maven.apache.org/maven-v4_0_0.xsd">
  <modelVersion>4.0.0</modelVersion>
  <parent>
    <groupId>com.packt.androidMaven</groupId>
    <artifactId>chapter5</artifactId>
    <version>1.0-SNAPSHOT</version>
  </parent>
  <artifactId>FreeVersion</artifactId>
  <packaging>apk</packaging>
  <name>Free Version</name>

  <dependencies>
    <dependency>
      <groupId>com.google.android</groupId>
      <artifactId>android</artifactId>
      <scope>provided</scope>
    </dependency>
    <dependency>
      <groupId>${project.groupId}</groupId>
      <artifactId>CommonLibrary</artifactId>
      <version>${project.version}</version>
```

```
        <type>aar</type>
      </dependency>
    </dependencies>
  </project>
```

The only tricky part is that we need to include the common library in the dependencies section by providing the Maven dependency and specifying its type to be AAR.

Our next step is to write down the manifest files for each module. Android libraries need a manifest file, but since these projects cannot be deployed to a device, we can omit some configuration and move it directly to the actual Android projects.

Our example is almost identical to what we have seen so far. The common library contains two activities, the main activity and an activity that is common/free to all versions. So, all we need to do is to register these activities to the manifest file, as shown in the next code snippet:

```xml
<?xml version="1.0" encoding="utf-8"?>
<manifest
xmlns:android="http://schemas.android.com/apk/res/android"
package="com.packt.androidmaven.common"
android:versionCode="1"
android:versionName="1.0-SNAPSHOT"
xmlns:xsi="http://www.w3.org/2001/XMLSchema-instance"
xsi:schemaLocation="http://schemas.android.com/apk/res/android ">
  <application>
    <activity android:name=".MainActivity" >
      <intent-filter>
        <action android:name="android.intent.action.MAIN" />
        <category android:name="android.intent.category.LAUNCHER"
        />
      </intent-filter>
    </activity>
    <activity android:name=".FreeActivity" >
    </activity>
  </application>
</manifest>
```

Since this is an Android Library project, it's clear that we don't need to specify the application's icon, label, or theme like we did before, because this library project will not be deployed in a device. Registering the activities is more than enough. Here's the code of the two activities included in the shared library, CommonLibrary module:

```java
package com.packt.androidmaven.common;

import android.app.Activity;
import android.os.Bundle;
```

```
import android.widget.TextView;

public class FreeActivity extends Activity {
  @Override
  public void onCreate(Bundle savedInstanceState) {
    super.onCreate(savedInstanceState);
    TextView textView = new TextView(this);
    textView.setTextSize(40);
    textView.setText("Hey I'm a free activity!");
    setContentView(textView);
  }
}

package com.packt.androidmaven.common;

import android.app.Activity;
import android.content.ActivityNotFoundException;
import android.content.Intent;
import android.os.Bundle;
import android.view.View;
import android.view.View.OnClickListener;
import android.widget.Button;
import android.widget.TextView;
import android.widget.Toast;
import static android.widget.Toast.LENGTH_SHORT;

public class MainActivity extends Activity {
  private Button button;
  private TextView textView;

  @Override
  public void onCreate(Bundle savedInstanceState) {
    super.onCreate(savedInstanceState);
    setContentView(R.layout.activity_main);
    setTextValue();
    addListenerOnButton();
    addListenerOnPaidButton();
  }

  private void setTextValue() {
    textView = (TextView) findViewById(R.id.text1);
    textView.setText("Main Activity");
  }

  public void addListenerOnButton() {
    button = (Button) findViewById(R.id.button1);
    button.setOnClickListener(new OnClickListener() {
```

```
      @Override
      public void onClick(View view) {
        Intent intent = new Intent(view.getContext(),
        FreeActivity.class);
        startActivity(intent);
      }
    });
  }

  public void addListenerOnPaidButton() {
    button = (Button) findViewById(R.id.paidbutton);
    button.setOnClickListener(new OnClickListener() {
      @Override
      public void onClick(View view) {
        try {
          Intent intent = new Intent();
          intent.setAction("com.packt.paid.intent.action.Launch");
          startActivity(intent);
        }
        catch (ActivityNotFoundException e) {
          Toast.makeText(view.getContext(), "You need to purchase
          the full version!", LENGTH_SHORT).show();
        }
      }
    });
  }
}
```

Bear in mind, also, that typical resource files like activities configurations, string resources, and so on can and should be contained in this project for all the shared Android components included in this module so that the other modules won't need to include. This will avoid code and configuration duplication and will make the development and release management much easier. However, you can always override a property, a string, or anything else located under the res directory. A typical case is to provide different icons or different application name for the paid and free versions. You can have a default one in the common library and override it in the corresponding Maven modules.

Now, let's see how the manifest files of our actual projects look like, starting with the one located inside the free version:

```
<?xml version="1.0" encoding="utf-8"?>
<manifest
xmlns:android="http://schemas.android.com/apk/res/android"
package="com.packt.androidmaven.free"
android:versionCode="1"
```

```
android:versionName="1.0-SNAPSHOT"
xmlns:xsi="http://www.w3.org/2001/XMLSchema-instance"
xsi:schemaLocation="http://schemas.android.com/apk/res/android ">
  <application android:icon="@drawable/ic_launcher"
    android:label="@string/app_name"
    android:theme="@style/AppTheme">
    <activity
    android:name="com.packt.androidmaven.common.MainActivity" >
      <intent-filter>
        <action android:name="android.intent.action.MAIN" />
        <category android:name="android.intent.category.LAUNCHER"
        />
      </intent-filter>
    </activity>
    <activity
    android:name="com.packt.androidmaven.common.FreeActivity" >
    </activity>
  </application>
</manifest>
```

The key point here is that we need to declare in the manifest file of the application project all components that will be referenced and are imported from the common library. This includes all activities, services, providers, as well as permissions. Bear in mind that any reference to a library component should be done by using the fully qualified package name. For instance in the previous example shown, we need to reference both activities included in the common library, and so we use the complete package name in their declaration.

Another good practice is to have different package name in the application projects than the one used in the library project. But wait a minute? Wouldn't this cause the problems we have discussed several times throughout this chapter? How our classes will make use of the R.java class if we have different package names? Well, that's the beauty of this approach. The classes included in the common library are compiled with their package name and uses the original R.java class. The code located in the application projects can use both R.java classes, the one imported from the common library dependency and the one generated in the target project during compile time. No more dynamic change of the package name. We have a clearer and more robust solution here.

Going back to the manifest file of the free version module, you can see that we don't register any new activities because, in our example, our simple free version uses only the activities imported by the shared library:

```
<?xml version="1.0" encoding="utf-8"?>

<manifest
xmlns:android="http://schemas.android.com/apk/res/android"
package="com.packt.androidmaven.paid"
android:versionCode="1"
android:versionName="1.0-SNAPSHOT"
xmlns:xsi="http://www.w3.org/2001/XMLSchema-instance"
xsi:schemaLocation="http://schemas.android.com/apk/res/android ">
  <application android:icon="@drawable/ic_launcher"
  android:label="@string/app_name"
  android:theme="@style/AppTheme">
    <activity
    android:name="com.packt.androidmaven.common.MainActivity" >
      <intent-filter>
        <action android:name="android.intent.action.MAIN" />
        <category android:name="android.intent.category.LAUNCHER"
        />
      </intent-filter>
    </activity>
    <activity
    android:name="com.packt.androidmaven.common.FreeActivity" >
    </activity>
  </application>
</manifest>
```

On the other hand, the paid version needs to register a new activity, `PaidActivity.java`. The one that is only available in this version. The manifest is very similar to the one we described for the free version, and in addition it contains the necessary declaration of this activity. You can see the differences in the highlighted section of the following configuration snippet:

```
<?xml version="1.0" encoding="utf-8"?>
<manifest
xmlns:android="http://schemas.android.com/apk/res/android"
package="com.packt.androidmaven.paid"
android:versionCode="1"
android:versionName="1.0-SNAPSHOT"
xmlns:xsi="http://www.w3.org/2001/XMLSchema-instance"
xsi:schemaLocation="http://schemas.android.com/apk/res/android ">
  <application android:icon="@drawable/ic_launcher"
    android:label="@string/app_name"
    android:theme="@style/AppTheme">
    <activity
    android:name="com.packt.androidmaven.common.MainActivity" >
```

```
      <intent-filter>
        <action android:name="android.intent.action.MAIN" />
        <category android:name="android.intent.category.LAUNCHER"
        />
      </intent-filter>
    </activity>
    <activity
    android:name="com.packt.androidmaven.common.FreeActivity" >
    </activity>
    <activity android:name=".PaidActivity" >
      <intent-filter>
        <action android:name="com.packt.paid.intent.action.Launch" />
        <category android:name="android.intent.category.DEFAULT" />
      </intent-filter>
    </activity>
  </application>
</manifest>
```

Like we said earlier, we won't list here the rest of the files of these projects source code, resources files, and so on, as they are similar to the files we have presented earlier in this book. They are always available in this GitHub project we already mentioned. Our goal is to make sure that you understand the important parts of this approach which are:

- Correct modularization
- Utilization of Android library
- Proper registration of all Android components in the manifest files

We are now ready to see our build configuration in action. First, we need to build the whole project. Open a terminal window and execute the following command:

```
mvn clean package
```

Then, let's install the free version in a device/emulator and verify that we don't have access to the restricted activity. Navigate to the `FreeVersion` directory, make sure that at least one device is connected or an emulator is running and deploy the free version of our application:

```
mvn android:deploy
```

 It's a good idea to completely uninstall all book example applications you have already installed in your device/emulator.

Now open the installed application—you will find it under the name **Free Version**—and try to click on the two buttons appearing in the initial screen. The first one should work and display a simple message in a new activity. The second one, however, should only display a toast message. The following image illustrates the expected behavior when clicking the buttons:

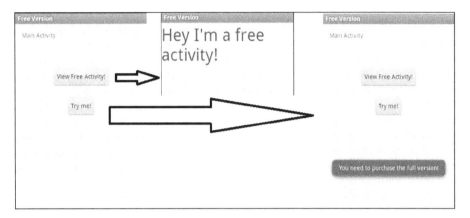

Go back to the terminal window and run the same command inside the PaidVersion directory to deploy the paid version. Check again your device/emulator and you will notice that there are two icons, as shown in the following image:

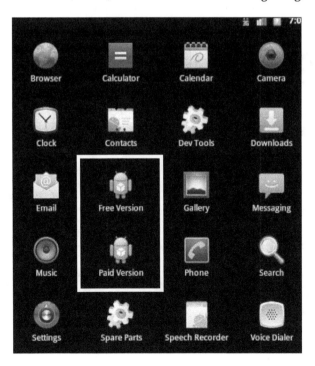

Now, start the paid version, and click again on the **Try me!** button. Et voila! The paid feature is now active and available to the user who just "purchased" our application!

You might also notice that when both applications are installed, the button from the free version will also display the thank you message, launching the activity from the paid application. This is because the paid version installation "unlocks" all paid features and so even the paid version can see them.

One last thing before we finish this chapter. We discussed two Maven alternatives to handle multiple versions of the same application. Both of them work fine and require some Maven configuration. If you ask our opinion, we would go with the second one. It's cleaner, more structured, and the Maven commands to deploy each version are much simpler.

Summary

This was one of the most challenging chapters we have written, and at the same time the most demanding one when talking to Android developers. We have stated one of the biggest problems that Android development teams face when we want to manage the development and build more than one version of the same application. We focused on providing real value to the scenario of an application with two versions: one free with limited features and one paid with all features available.

We provided two plans for making our Maven builds parameterized, and we explained in detail all the essential steps to get you from zero to a complete build configuration. Now that we have finished this chapter, we expect that you are familiar enough to:

- Have a basic idea of how Maven profiles work and their purpose
- Tell the differences between the two ways we discussed for developing more than one flavor of the same application

- Configure Maven to build all versions without manually modifying code, configuration files, or other resource files each time you want to build the project

- Understand why an Android library project provides a better structure and modularization in applications that need to have several versions, paid, free, and so on

What is coming next? You will learn how to properly package and deploy the application following Android suggested practices using the descriptive Maven-way.

6
Release Life Cycle and Continuous Integration

We are reaching the end of this book, but we still have some very important topics to cover. So far, we have prepared our development environment, we have set up our project structure, we learned how to write different type of tests, and we saw how to support multiple versions of the same Android application. All the above have been made easy with a declarative way using Maven configuration files and various Maven plugins.

Our Android application is now ready to be released and delivered to our customers. This chapter will guide you how to prepare the release of an application. We will also discuss how to deploy the application to an in-house repository for internal use and all the necessary steps to correctly prepare the APK package. Unfortunately, deploying an application to Android Market/Google Play using Maven is not yet available. Google released the first version of the publishing API (https://developers.google.com/android-publisher/#publishing) in July 2014 but there's no Maven plugin, to automate the process. The authors of this book have started working on such a plugin but due to time constraints it was not ready at the time this book was published. We will end this chapter by discussing a strategy of **Continuous Integration** (CI) that will allow you to automate the build, release, and deployment process. The topics that we will explore in this chapter are:

- Securing a package using a private key
- Obfuscating our code to protect from reverse engineering
- Zipalign the package
- Perform a release
- Deploy to a self-hosted repository
- Automation best practices

Optimizing an Android package

Google has well-defined a set of steps during the packaging and releasing phases of an Android application to ensure authenticity, optimization, and security. There are three suggested practices: sign, obfuscate, and zipalign. The first one is always performed automatically by the Android build system, even if we don't explicitly describe it in Maven configuration and specify a custom key. The other two are optional, but highly recommended for all Android developers.

In this section of the chapter, we will briefly explain the purpose of each step, and then we will discuss how we can configure Maven to run these tasks in a well-structured way like we have already done in all previous examples.

Signing an application

Like we said, Android requires that all packages, in order to be valid for installation in devices, need to be digitally signed with a certificate. This certificate is used by the Android ecosystem to validate the author of the application. Thankfully, the certificate is not required to be issued by a certificate authority. It would be a total nightmare for every Android developer and it would increase the cost of developing applications. However, if you want to sign the certificate by a trusted authority like the majority of the certificates used in web servers, you are free to do it.

One might wonder *It's the first time we talk about certificates and signing process prior to installation, but throughout this book we have installed numerous times various applications in devices and/or emulators. How did this happen since we haven't signed anything?*

Android supports two modes of signing: debug and release. Debug mode is used by default during the development of the application, and the release mode when we are ready to release and publish it. In debug mode, when building and packaging an application the Android SDK automatically generates a certificate and signs the package. So don't worry; even though we haven't told Maven to do anything about signing, Android knows what to do and behind the scenes signs the package with the autogenerated key.

When it comes to distributing an application, debug mode is not enough; so, we need to prepare our own self-signed certificate and instruct Maven to use it instead of the default one. Before we dive to Maven configuration, let us quickly remind you how to issue your own certificate. Open a command window, and type the following command:

```
keytool -genkey -v -keystore my-android-release-key.keystore -alias my-android-key -keyalg RSA -keysize 2048 -validity 10000
```

If the `keytool` command line utility is not in your path, then it's a good idea to add it. It's located under the `%JAVA_HOME%/bin` directory. Alternatively, you can execute the command inside this directory. Let us explain some parameters of this command. We use the `keytool` command line utility to create a new `keystore` file under the name `my-android-release-key.keystore` inside the current directory. The `-alias` parameter is used to define an alias name for this key, and it will be used later on in Maven configuration. We also specify the algorithm, RSA, and the key size, 2048; finally we set the validity period in days. In our example, the generated key will be valid for 10,000 days — long enough for many many new versions of our application!

After running the command, you will be prompted to answer a series of questions like those shown in the following image:

```
Enter keystore password:
Re-enter new password:
What is your first and last name?
  [Unknown]:  Patroklos Papapetrou
What is the name of your organizational unit?
  [Unknown]:  Freelancer
What is the name of your organization?
  [Unknown]:  Freelancer
What is the name of your City or Locality?
  [Unknown]:  Thessaloniki
What is the name of your State or Province?
  [Unknown]:  Macedonia
What is the two-letter country code for this unit?
  [Unknown]:  GR
Is CN=Patroklos Papapetrou, OU=Freelancer, O=Freelancer, L=Thessaloniki, ST=Macedonia, C=GR correct?
  [no]:  yes

Generating 2,048 bit RSA key pair and self-signed certificate (SHA256withRSA) with a validity of 10,000 days
    for: CN=Patroklos Papapetrou, OU=Freelancer, O=Freelancer, L=Thessaloniki, ST=Macedonia, C=GR
Enter key password for <my-android-key2>
    (RETURN if same as keystore password):
[Storing my-android-release-key2.keystore]
```

First, type twice a password for the `keystore` file. It's a good idea to note it down because we will use it again in our Maven configuration. For the purposes of our example, type the word :**secret** in both prompts. Then, we need to provide some identification data, like name, surname, organization details, and location. Finally, we need to set a password for the key. If we want to keep the same password with the `keystore` file, we can just hit *RETURN*.

If everything goes well, we will see the final message that informs us that the key is being stored in the `keystore` file with the name we just defined. After this, our key is ready to be used to sign our Android application.

> The key used in debug mode can be found in this file: `~/.android.debug.keystore` and contains the following information:
>
> ```
> Keystore name: "debug.keystore"
> Keystore password: "android"
> Key alias: "androiddebugkey"
> Key password: "android"
> CN: "CN=Android Debug,O=Android,C=US"
> ```

Now, it's time to let Maven use the key we just generated. We will again use in this chapter, the example we presented in *Chapter 5, Android Flavors* — the multimodule Android project with one paid and one free version. Before we add the necessary configuration to our pom.xml file, we need to add a Maven profile to the global Maven settings. Recall from the previous chapter that profiles defined in the user settings.xml file can be used by all Maven projects in the same machine. This file is usually located under this folder: %M2_HOME%/conf/settings.xml. One fundamental advantage of defining global profiles in user's Maven settings is that this configuration is not shared in the pom.xml file to all developers that work on the application. The settings.xml file should never be kept under the **Source Control Management (SCM)** tool. Users can safely enter personal or critical information like passwords and keys, which is exactly the case of our example.

Now, edit the settings.xml file and add the following lines inside the <profiles> attribute:

```
<profile>
  <id>release</id>
  <properties>
    <sign.keystore>/path/to/my/keystore/my-android-release-
    key.keystore</sign.keystore>
    <sign.alias>my-android-key</sign.alias>
    <sign.storepass>secret</sign.storepass>
    <sign.keypass>secret</sign.keypass>
  </properties>
</profile>
```

Keep in mind that the keystore name, the alias name, the keystore password, and the key password should be the ones we used when we created the keystore file.

> Clearly, storing passwords in plain text, even in a file that is normally protected from other users, is not a very good practice. A quick way to make it slightly less easy to read the password is to use XML entities to write the value. Some sites on the internet like this one http://coderstoolbox.net/string/#!encoding=xml&action=encode&charset=none provide such encryptions.
>
> It will be resolved as plain text when the file is loaded; so Maven won't even notice it. In this case, this would become:
>
> ```
> <sign.storepass>&#115;&#101;&#99;&#114;&#101;&#116;</
> sign.storepass>
> ```

We have prepared our global profile and the corresponding properties, and so we can now edit the `pom.xml` file of the parent project and do the proper configuration. Adding common configuration in the parent file for all Maven submodules is a good practice in our case because at some point, we would like to release both free and paid versions, and it's preferable to avoid duplicating the same configuration in two files.

We want to create a new profile and add all the necessary settings there, because the release process is not something that runs every day during the development phase. It should run only at a final stage, when we are ready to deploy our application. Our first priority is to tell Maven to disable debug mode. Then, we need to specify a new Maven plugin name `:maven-jarsigner-plugin`, which is responsible for driving the verification and signing process for custom/private certificates. You can find the complete release profile as follows:

```xml
<profiles>
  <profile>
    <id>release</id>
    <build>
      <plugins>
        <plugin>
          <groupId>com.jayway.maven.plugins.android.generation2
          </groupId>
          <artifactId>android-maven-plugin</artifactId>
          <extensions>true</extensions>
          <configuration>
            <sdk>
              <platform>19</platform>
            </sdk>
            <sign>
              <debug>false</debug>
            </sign>
          </configuration>
        </plugin>
        <plugin>
          <groupId>org.apache.maven.plugins</groupId>
          <artifactId>maven-jarsigner-plugin</artifactId>
          <executions>
            <execution>
              <id>signing</id>
              <phase>package</phase>
              <goals>
                <goal>sign</goal>
                <goal>verify</goal>
              </goals>
```

```
                    <inherited>true</inherited>
                    <configuration>
                      <removeExistingSignatures>true
                      </removeExistingSignatures>
                      <archiveDirectory />
                      <includes>
                        <include>${project.build.directory}/
                        ${project.artifactId}.apk</include>
                      </includes>
                      <keystore>${sign.keystore}</keystore>
                      <alias>${sign.alias}</alias>
                      <storepass>${sign.storepass}</storepass>
                      <keypass>${sign.keypass}</keypass>
                      <verbose>true</verbose>
                    </configuration>
                  </execution>
                </executions>
              </plugin>
            </plugins>
          </build>
        </profile>
      </profiles>
```

We instruct the JAR signer plugin to be triggered during the package phase and run the goals of verification and signing. Furthermore, we tell the plugin to remove any existing signatures from the package and use the variable values we have defined in our global profile, $sign.alias, $sign.keystore, $sign.storepass and $sign. keypass. The "verbose" setting is used here to verify that the private key is used instead of the debug key.

Before we run our new profile, for comparison purposes, let's package our application without using the signing capability. Open a terminal window, and type the following Maven command:

`mvn clean package`

When the command finishes, navigate to the paid version target directory, /PaidVersion/target, and take a look at its contents. You will notice that there are two packaging files: a PaidVersion.jar (size 14KB) and PaidVersion.apk (size 46KB).

Since we haven't discussed yet about releasing an application, we can just run the following command in a terminal window and see how the private key is used for signing the package:

`mvn clean package -Prelease`

You must have probably noticed that we use only one profile name, and that is the beauty of Maven. Profiles with the same ID are merged together, and so it's easier to understand and maintain the build scripts.

If you want to double-check that the package is signed with your private certificate, you can monitor the Maven output, and at some point you will see something similar to the following image:

```
[INFO] s k    2815 Wed Dec 31 20:46:00 EET 2014 META-INF/MANIFEST.MF
[INFO]         2914 Wed Dec 31 20:46:00 EET 2014 META-INF/MY-ANDRO.SF
[INFO]         1400 Wed Dec 31 20:46:00 EET 2014 META-INF/MY-ANDRO.RSA
[INFO]            0 Wed Dec 31 20:46:00 EET 2014 META-INF/
[INFO]            0 Wed Dec 31 20:46:00 EET 2014 META-INF/maven/
[INFO]            0 Wed Dec 31 20:46:00 EET 2014 META-INF/maven/com.packt.androidMaven/
[INFO]            0 Wed Dec 31 20:46:00 EET 2014 META-INF/maven/com.packt.androidMaven/PaidVersion/
[INFO]            0 Wed Dec 31 20:46:00 EET 2014 com/
[INFO]            0 Wed Dec 31 20:46:00 EET 2014 com/packt/
[INFO]            0 Wed Dec 31 20:46:00 EET 2014 com/packt/androidmaven/
[INFO]            0 Wed Dec 31 20:46:00 EET 2014 com/packt/androidmaven/common/
[INFO]            0 Wed Dec 31 20:46:00 EET 2014 com/packt/androidmaven/paid/
[INFO] smk     997 Wed Dec 31 20:46:00 EET 2014 META-INF/maven/com.packt.androidMaven/PaidVersion/pom.xml
[INFO] smk     130 Wed Dec 31 20:46:00 EET 2014 META-INF/maven/com.packt.androidMaven/PaidVersion/pom.properties
[INFO] smk     819 Wed Dec 31 20:46:00 EET 2014 com/packt/androidmaven/common/FreeActivity.class
[INFO] smk    1132 Wed Dec 31 20:46:00 EET 2014 com/packt/androidmaven/common/MainActivity$1.class
[INFO] smk    1510 Wed Dec 31 20:46:00 EET 2014 com/packt/androidmaven/common/MainActivity$2.class
[INFO] smk    1822 Wed Dec 31 20:46:00 EET 2014 com/packt/androidmaven/common/MainActivity.class
[INFO] smk     494 Wed Dec 31 20:46:00 EET 2014 com/packt/androidmaven/common/R$dimen.class
[INFO] smk     440 Wed Dec 31 20:46:00 EET 2014 com/packt/androidmaven/common/R$drawable.class
[INFO] smk     481 Wed Dec 31 20:46:00 EET 2014 com/packt/androidmaven/common/R$id.class
[INFO] smk     436 Wed Dec 31 20:46:00 EET 2014 com/packt/androidmaven/common/R$layout.class
[INFO] smk     508 Wed Dec 31 20:46:00 EET 2014 com/packt/androidmaven/common/R$string.class
[INFO] smk     464 Wed Dec 31 20:46:00 EET 2014 com/packt/androidmaven/common/R$style.class
[INFO] smk     673 Wed Dec 31 20:46:00 EET 2014 com/packt/androidmaven/common/R.class
[INFO] smk     363 Wed Dec 31 20:46:00 EET 2014 com/packt/androidmaven/paid/BuildConfig.class
[INFO] smk     823 Wed Dec 31 20:46:00 EET 2014 com/packt/androidmaven/paid/PaidActivity.class
[INFO] smk     367 Wed Dec 31 20:46:00 EET 2014 com/packt/androidmaven/paid/R$attr.class
[INFO] smk     488 Wed Dec 31 20:46:00 EET 2014 com/packt/androidmaven/paid/R$dimen.class
[INFO] smk     434 Wed Dec 31 20:46:00 EET 2014 com/packt/androidmaven/paid/R$drawable.class
[INFO] smk     475 Wed Dec 31 20:46:00 EET 2014 com/packt/androidmaven/paid/R$id.class
[INFO] smk     430 Wed Dec 31 20:46:00 EET 2014 com/packt/androidmaven/paid/R$layout.class
[INFO] smk     534 Wed Dec 31 20:46:00 EET 2014 com/packt/androidmaven/paid/R$string.class
[INFO] smk     458 Wed Dec 31 20:46:00 EET 2014 com/packt/androidmaven/paid/R$style.class
[INFO] smk     712 Wed Dec 31 20:46:00 EET 2014 com/packt/androidmaven/paid/R.class
[INFO]
[INFO]
[INFO]   s = signature was verified
[INFO]   m = entry is listed in manifest
[INFO]   k = at least one certificate was found in keystore
[INFO]   i = at least one certificate was found in identity scope
[INFO]   X = not signed by specified alias(es)
```

This output verifies that the classes have been properly signed through the execution of the Maven JAR signer plugin.

To better understand how signing and optimization affects the packages generation, we can navigate again to the /PaidVersion/target directory and take a look at the files created. You will be surprised to see that the same packages exist again but they have different sizes. The PaidVersion.jar file has a size of 18KB, which is greater than the file generated without signing. However, the PaidVersion.apk is smaller (size 44KB) than the first version. These differences happen because the .jar file is signed with the new certificate; so the size is getting slightly bigger, but what about the .apk file. Should be also bigger because every file is signed with the certificate.

The answer can be easily found if we open both the .apk files and compare them. They are compressed files so any well-known tool that opens compressed files can do this. If you take a closer look at the contents of the .apk files, you will notice that the contents of the .apk file that was generated using the private certificate are slightly larger except the resources.arsc file. This file, in the case of custom signing, is compressed, whereas in the debug signing mode it is in raw format. This explains why the signed version of the .apk file is smaller than the original one.

There's also one last thing that verifies the correct completion of signing.
Keep the compressed .apk files opened and navigate to the META-INF directory.
These directories contain a couple of different files, and this is illustrated in the
following image:

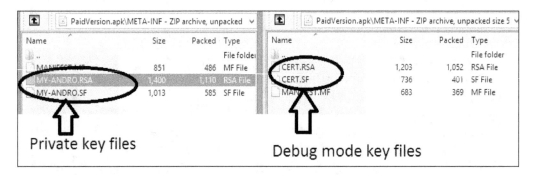

The signed package with our personal certificate contains the key files named with
the alias we used when we created the certificate and the package signed in debug
mode contains the default certificate used by Android.

Later on in this chapter, we will see how the rest of the tools we will discuss affects
the size and contents of the .apk files.

Obfuscating the code

The next step is to obfuscate our code. **Obfuscation** is a practice that is available to
many programming languages. Its purpose is to make hard, really hard for potential
hackers to reverse-engineer your code. Android natively supports obfuscation
through a tool called **ProGuard**. This tool will remove unused code and will rename
all classes, attributes, and methods using some obscure names. It will also produce
a smaller .apk file because it shrinks and optimizes the code. Like we said, using
ProGuard is completely optional, but we strongly recommend it, especially when
your application uses security-sensitive features.

Following Android's practice, the android-Maven plugin doesn't activate the
ProGuard by default, so we need to explicitly enable it. This is pretty straightforward
by adding the <proguard> attribute inside the configuration section and set the skip
flag to False. After this change, the android-Maven plugin should look like this:

```
<plugin>
    <groupId>com.jayway.maven.plugins.android.generation2</groupId>
    <artifactId>android-maven-plugin</artifactId>
    <extensions>true</extensions>
    <configuration>
```

```
    <sdk>
      <platform>19</platform>
    </sdk>
    <sign>
      <debug>false</debug>
    </sign>
    <proguard>
      <skip>false</skip>
    </proguard>
  </configuration>
</plugin>
```

If we try to again package our application, we will notice that ProGuard is not running and instead we see the following message in Maven log:

Proguard skipped because the configuration file doesn't exist:

PATH/TO/MAVEN/PROJECT/proguard.cfg

So, we have to create that file and properly configure it. Explaining all the details of ProGuard and the available properties is out of the context of this book; so, we will just provide a suggested configuration for every Android project. Here are the typical contents of a `proguard.cfg` file. Make sure that the same file exists under every module directory:

```
-optimizationpasses 5
-dontusemixedcaseclassnames
-dontskipnonpubliclibraryclasses
-dontpreverify
-verbose
-optimizations
!code/simplification/arithmetic,!field/*,!class/merging/*

-keep public class * extends android.app.Activity
-keep public class * extends android.app.Application
-keep public class * extends android.app.Service
-keep public class * extends android.content.BroadcastReceiver
-keep public class * extends android.content.ContentProvider
-keep public class * extends android.app.backup.BackupAgentHelper
-keep public class * extends android.preference.Preference
-keep public class com.android.vending.licensing.ILicensingService

-keepclasseswithmembernames class * {
  native <methods>;
}
```

```
-keepclasseswithmembers class * {
  public <init>(android.content.Context,
  android.util.AttributeSet);
}

-keepclasseswithmembers class * {
  public <init>(android.content.Context,
  android.util.AttributeSet, int);
}

-keepclassmembers class * extends android.app.Activity {
  public void *(android.view.View);
}

-keepclassmembers enum * {
  public static **[] values();
  public static ** valueOf(java.lang.String);
}

-keep class * implements android.os.Parcelable {
  public static final android.os.Parcelable$Creator *;
}

# adding this in to preserve line numbers so that the stack traces
# can be remapped
-renamesourcefileattribute SourceFile
-keepattributes SourceFile,LineNumberTable
```

 Android SDK comes with a default ProGuard file to be used as a starting point. It is named `proguard-android.txt` and it can be found under the `/tools/proguard` folder.

If you want to read more about ProGuard features or use it for other non-Android projects, you can visit the official web page here: `http://proguard.sourceforge.net`

Before we explain the last part of the optimizing process, we can compare again the generated files. Looking at `/PaidVersion/target` directory after obfuscating the packages, we notice that the `.apk` file is smaller and has a size of 43KB. This is expected because, like we already discussed, during obfuscation all unused codes are removed. Take a look at the following screenshot:

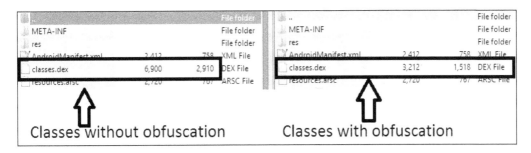

Classes without obfuscation   Classes with obfuscation

The preceding image illustrates that the compiled application code, classes.dex, is much smaller after obfuscation. The file has been reduced more than half of its size before compression. This size reduction is more obvious in applications with larger code bases than our little example.

Aligning and zipping uncompressed data

The last thing we need to take care during Android packaging is to optimize the produced .apk files. Android SDK uses a tool called **zipalign** that applies an alignment and zipping algorithm to the package; so, the total amount of memory consumed when the application runs in a device is heavily reduced. Practically, behind the scenes, zipalign makes sure that all uncompressed data like images or raw files are aligned on 4-byte boundaries, which makes their access more efficient during runtime using nmap() method.

Android advises that the tool is always used before packaging the application for distribution. For development and debugging purposes, alignment is not necessary; so, we will add all configurations needed in the "release" profile.

It is important that the alignment and compression of the .package file are done only after signing the .apk file with the private key. Doing zipalign before signing won't have any effect because the signing procedure will undo the alignment. Finally, bear in mind that making changes to the aligned package is not recommended, because this will cause disruption of the changed entries and all later entries. This practically means that the package will not be aligned any more.

To do so, we will modify the configuration of the android-Maven plugin. First, we need to enable the zipalign task in the parent `pom.xml` file. This is easily done in the same way we enabled ProGuard in the previous section. In the `<configuration>` element, we add the `<zipalign>` element and we set the `skip` property to `False`. Moreover, we can describe the names of the input and output APK package. After this, we should tell the plugin to execute zipalign during the packaging phase. The results of these changes are shown in the following code snippet. The bold letters highlight the changes we did for the zipalign task;

```
<plugin>
  <groupId>com.jayway.maven.plugins.android.generation2</groupId>
  <artifactId>android-maven-plugin</artifactId>
  <extensions>true</extensions>
  <configuration>
    <sdk>
      <platform>19</platform>
    </sdk>
    <sign>
      <debug>false</debug>
    </sign>
    <proguard>
      <skip>false</skip>
    </proguard>
    <zipalign>
      <skip>false</skip>
      <verbose>true</verbose>
      <inputApk>${project.build.directory}/${project.artifactId}.apk
      </inputApk>
      <outputApk>${project.build.directory}/${project.artifactId}-
      signed-aligned.apk</outputApk>
    </zipalign>
  </configuration>
  <executions>
    <execution>
      <id>alignApk</id>
      <phase>package</phase>
      <goals>
        <goal>zipalign</goal>
      </goals>
    </execution>
  </executions>
</plugin>
```

Let's run once again in a terminal window the Maven packaging goal of our project with the two `release` profiles:

```
mvn clean package -Prelease
```

Navigate to the `/PaidVersion/target` directory, and you will observe that there's a new `.apk` file named `PaidVersion-signed-aligned`. This is the file name we have instructed the android-Maven plugin to give to the generated packaged after alignment, and so everything works as expected.

Transforming the package in shippable form

Well done! So far, we have properly configured our Maven `pom.xml` file to sign, obfuscate, and align the application package, but still we are not ready to deploy. Maven deploys the target packages to repositories (local or remote) but the extension of Android packages, `.apk` file, is not understood as a valid package file; so, it will probably be rejected during deployment. The build-helper plugin comes to the rescue and can transform our package to a shippable form — to a file that can be accepted by a Maven repository.

All we need to do is to add the plugin configuration to our `release` profile and execute the `attach-artifact` goal during the packaging phase:

```xml
<plugin>
  <groupId>org.codehaus.mojo</groupId>
  <artifactId>build-helper-maven-plugin</artifactId>
  <configuration>
    <artifacts>
      <artifact>
        <file>${project.build.directory}/${project.artifactId}-
        signed-aligned.apk</file>
        <type>apk</type>
        <classifier>signed-aligned</classifier>
      </artifact>
    </artifacts>
  </configuration>
  <executions>
    <execution>
      <id>attach-signed-aligned</id>
      <phase>package</phase>
      <goals>
        <goal>attach-artifact</goal>
      </goals>
    </execution>
  </executions>
</plugin>
```

As shown in the preceding code snippet, first we develop the artifact that we want to deploy to a Maven repository. In our case, the artifact is the package generated after signing and aligning. Then, we add an execution element and we invoke the attach-artifact goal. Now, we are ready for the final step and perform a release of our application.

Releasing a new version

Although performing a release usually is followed by deploying the packages to a Maven repository, it is not always required. This practically means that you can just release an application or distribute it manually to its users.

The release process is supported by the Maven-release plugin, but we need to make sure that the following requirements are met:

- Although this is optional, it is highly recommended to explicitly define the version of the Maven-release plugin in the `<pluginManagement>` element of the `pom.xml` file

- The SCM URL that points to the folder containing the `pom.xml` file is correctly configured in the `<scm>` section of the `pom.xml` file

- There are no pending local modifications to be committed. Otherwise, the plugin will display an error message.

The URL is prefixed with `scm:[scm-provider]` parameter. This way, the plugin can execute the correct commands, behind the scenes, to commit changes of the `pom.xml` file and do the tagging. For more information on how to configure your favorite SCM, you can visit this page: `http://maven.apache.org/scm/scms-overview.html`.

In the next two sections, we will first cover the details of releasing a new version without deploying it to a local or remote repository, and then we will guide you through the process of installing a local repository, Artifactory, and deploy the released version to this repository.

Perform a release without deployment to repository

Let's configure our application with the proper settings we just explained. First, we will add the version of the Maven-release plugin in our parent `pom.xml` file. To do so, just add the following code snippet in the boundaries of the `<pluginManagement>` element:

```
<plugin>
  <groupId>org.apache.maven.plugins</groupId>
  <artifactId>maven-release-plugin</artifactId>
  <version>2.5.1</version>
</plugin>
```

Then, add the next code snippet as part of the root element of the `pom.xml` file:

```
<scm>
  <developerConnection>
    scm:git:https://github.com/ppapapetrou76/
    AndroidMavenDevelopment/tree/master/Chapter6
  </developerConnection>
</scm>
```

Now, we can briefly explain the steps to release the application. The process typically consists of two steps:

1. Prepare.
2. Perform PP.

First, we prepare the release by providing information such as the number of the next version, the tag name, and so on. Actually, this release prepare step is the actual release of the application without deploying it to a local or a remote repository. During this step, the Maven-release plugin will do the following:

1. Check that there are no uncommitted changes in the sources. It will raise an error if found.

2. Check that there are no SNAPSHOT dependencies. It will raise an error if found.

3. Change the version in the `pom.xml` files from 1.0-SNAPSHOT to the new version we will provide or the default one, 1.0.

4. Make changes the SCM information in the `pom.xml` file to include the final destination of the tag.

5. Commit the modified `pom.xml` files.

6. Tag the code in the SCM with the version name that we will provide.

7. Bump the version in the `pom.xml` files to a new value we will provide or the default one, that is, 1.1-SNAPSHOT.

 Commit the modified `pom.xml` files SNAPSHOT is a very special version qualifier. Maven treats it as a not-yet-released version of the current version number. In other words, it is generally considered as the development version. The "SNAPSHOT" qualifier, although not required, has become a standard for naming the development versions and it's the way we have followed so far through the examples of this book. The Maven-release plugin expects to find it in the version number, and requires a "clean" number version without such qualifier; this is why during the release process it suggests only the version number for the release.

Then, we can "perform" the release, which in practice means that the Maven-release plugin will:

- Check out from an SCM URL with optional tag.
- Run the predefined Maven goals to release the project. We will talk about them in the next section of this chapter.

Now, it's time to "prepare" our release. Open a terminal window and type the following command, in the directory where the parent `pom.xml` file is located, to prepare the release:

```
mvn release:prepare -Prelease
```

You will prompted to answer a bunch of questions, but you can accept the proposed value by just hitting *RETURN*, as shown in the following image:

```
What is the release version for "Chapter 6 - Release"? (com.packt.androidMaven:chapter6) 1.0: :
What is the release version for "CommonLibrary"? (com.packt.androidMaven:CommonLibrary) 1.0: :
What is the release version for "Free Version"? (com.packt.androidMaven:FreeVersion) 1.0: :
What is the release version for "Paid Version"? (com.packt.androidMaven:PaidVersion) 1.0: :
What is SCM release tag or label for "Chapter 6 - Release"? (com.packt.androidMaven:chapter6) chapter6-1.0: :
What is the new development version for "Chapter 6 - Release"? (com.packt.androidMaven:chapter6) 1.1-SNAPSHOT: :
What is the new development version for "CommonLibrary"? (com.packt.androidMaven:CommonLibrary) 1.1-SNAPSHOT: :
What is the new development version for "Free Version"? (com.packt.androidMaven:FreeVersion) 1.1-SNAPSHOT: :
What is the new development version for "Paid Version"? (com.packt.androidMaven:PaidVersion) 1.1-SNAPSHOT: :
```

When the Maven task is completed, you can examine the changes made in our `pom.xml` files. You will notice that all 1.0-SNAPSHOT versions have been replaced with 1.0, even in the dependencies of `CommonLibrary` module in the Maven configuration of `PaidVersion` and `FreeVersion` modules. The following line has also been added to the `<scm>` element:

```
<tag>chapter6-1.0</tag>
```

All changes have been pushed to the Git repository and a new tag with the name `chapter6-1.0` has been created. Hooray! We have just completed our release. Now, our `.apk` file can be manually distributed to our customers and we can continue working with the next development version, which in our case is 1.1-SNAPSHOT.

Deploying to a local repository

Clearly, distributing manually or keeping in a nonstandard way our release packages are not a good practice. Like we already said, normally all Maven artifacts created during the release process should be deployed in a Maven repository. Installing and configuring a Maven repository is out of the context of this book. However, if you don't have a Maven repository installed, we highly recommend that you download and install Artifactory, the most popular, free, and open source Maven repository management system.

Artifactory is a pure JEE standalone application. You can download the latest version at the website: `http://www.jfrog.com/open-source/` and you can find a very well-documented wiki that will guide you to the installation and setup process here: `https://www.jfrog.com/confluence/display/RTF/Installing+Artifactory`.

Normally, after finishing the installation and start-up Artifactory, you can access it by locally pointing your browser to this URL: `http://localhost:8081`.

Also keep in mind that the default credentials to log in are the following: `username = admin`, `password = password`

You can also download a ready-to-use Artifactory installation by downloading a Bitnami virtual machine: `https://bitnami.com/stack/artifactory`.

Before we try to deploy application package to the Maven repository, we need to make some final changes to our parent `pom.xml` file and tell Maven where is our Maven repository. In Maven configuration terms, this is called **Distribution Management**. The following code snippet should be copied inside the root element:

```
<distributionManagement>
  <repository>
    <id>internal.repo</id>
    <name>Android Internal repo</name>
    <url>http://localhost:8081/artifactory/libs-release-
    local</url>
  </repository>
</distributionManagement>
```

In the preceding example, we have used one of the predefined repositories that Artifactory is shipped with, like `libs-release-local` to host released artifacts, `libs-snapshot-local` to host snapshot artifacts, and so on.

If we try to perform the release using the following command line (notice that we don't need to specify the profiles any more because the packages are already generated and that the step only deploys them to the repository), we will receive a 401 error message (unauthorized):

`mvn release:perform`

This happens because every Maven repository does not allow artifact deployment without some basic authentication. Therefore, we will tell Maven which pair of username/password should use to access Artifactory. However, this would not be done in the `pom.xml` file but in the global Maven settings file because like we already pointed out, sensitive or/and not shareable information should not be kept in the `pom.xml` file. Edit the `%M2_HOME%/conf/settings.xml` file and add the following lines of code inside the `<servers>` element:

```
<server>
  <id>internal.repo2</id>
  <username>admin</username>
  <password>password</password>
</server>
```

 Maven provides a very elegant way of encrypting server passwords in `settings.exml` files. You can take a look at `http://maven.apache.org/guides/mini/guide-encryption.html` and if you want you can try to apply the instructions in our example.

Notice that the server ID in the global settings file and the repository ID in the project configuration file should be identical; otherwise, Maven will not be able to utilize them and access the repository to and deploy. Now, run again the release perform command and Maven should be able to successfully deploy the artifacts to the given repository.

To verify that everything has been published correctly, you can log in to the admin console of Artifactory and browse the `libs-release-local` repository as shown in the following image:

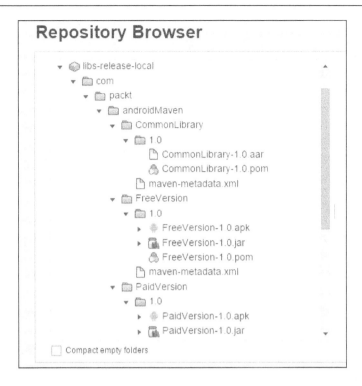

As illustrated in the preceding image, generated artifacts (JARs, APKs, and AARs) have been deployed to the repository. You notice also some files with .pom extension. These are the pom.xml files of our project renamed to be aligned with the names of the actual packages so that Maven can recognize them automatically.

There's one last thing that we want to share with you. You can achieve almost the same result of release and deploy without using the Maven-release plugin following these simple steps:

1. Manually change all versions from 1.0-SNAPSHOT to 1.0.
2. Push the code to the SCM repository.
3. Generate the artifacts by running this command on the parent directory
    mvn clean package -Prelease
4. Deploy the artifacts by running this command on the parent directory
    mvn deploy
5. Manually change all versions from 1.0 to 1.1-SNAPSHOT.
6. Push again the code to the SCM repository.

Technically, the only difference is that there's no tag creation. Everything else is exactly the same. Nevertheless, this approach is not recommended, because as we will see in the last section of this chapter, it requires manual changes of files and it cannot be easily automated.

Our packaging and deployment journey has to come to its end. We have created configuration settings for every step required or recommended by Android for a successful application release. The common characteristic of all steps is that it can be done by running a single Maven command without touching the code or other configuration files. Now, we are ready to move to the next level and automate everything to a robust and automated CI environment.

CI and automation best practices

CI is an agile practice that improves and facilitates software development processes. It requires developers to check-in the code frequently in a centralized source code repository. Every check-in triggers a new build job that—at least—compiles the code, runs unit tests, and builds the required artifacts (binaries, packages, and so on). This is the minimum set of activities that typically run on a CI environment. More sophisticated tasks, like nightly builds that run functional tests across different operating systems or different devices/emulators when living in the Android worlds, can also be achieved with proper configuration.

If setting up/using an SCM is considered as the "step A", when starting a new software development project, then setting up CI jobs is definitely the "step B". We can choose from a variety of open sources and commercial CI tools like **Jenkins** (`http://jenkins-ci.org`), **TeamCity** (`https://www.jetbrains.com/teamcity/`), **Travis** (`https://travis-ci.org/`), and **Bamboo** (`https://www.atlassian.com/software/bamboo`) just to mention the most popular ones. For simplicity, we will use in this section Jenkins CI. We regard it as the most easy to install and use; so even if you're not familiar enough with it, we are sure that you will easily follow our examples.

> There are several excellent articles and resources on the web about this that will explain in every detail the concept of CI and how developers should adopt. We highly recommend Martin Fowler's article `http://www.martinfowler.com/articles/continuousIntegration.html` and a couple of books available from Packt Publishing that focuses on popular CI tools like Jenkins and TeamCity.
>
> *Jenkins Continuous Integration Cookbook, Second Edition, Alan Mark Berg,* Packt Publishing.
>
> *Learning CI with TeamCity, Manoj Mahalingam,* Packt Publishing,

Downloading and installing Jenkins CI is really a piece of cake. Pick up the package for your local operating system and follow the installation guide found in this page: `https://wiki.jenkins-ci.org/display/JENKINS/Installing+Jenkins`. There, you should be able to access locally at port 8080, `http://localhost:8080`. By default, Jenkins does not require any user authentication and so you can perform all available actions we will show you in a minute.

Again, you can download a virtual machine with Jenkins installed and configured by **Btinami**:

`https://bitnami.com/stack/jenkins`

or turnkey:

`http://www.turnkeylinux.org/jenkins`

Before we explain the job creation, we will do some global configuration and tell Jenkins where Maven and Git Client are located. Make sure that you have the required plugin installed in your Jenkins installation. In our case, we need the Git Client plugin. You can manage Jenkins plugins if you click on the **Manage Jenkins** link located at the top-left menu of your screen, and then click on the **Manage Plugins** link.

If you are using other than Git SCM repository, you should do follow similar steps to configure client's location. Now, click again on the **Manage Jenkins** link, but this time click on the **Configure System** option, as shown in the following image:

In the administration page that you will be redirected, locate the **Git Installations** section and click on the **Add Git** button. Then, just enter the full path to Git Client and enter a description. The following image shows how the screen should look:

Do the same with your Maven installation. Locate the **Maven Installations** section and click on the **Add Maven** button. Then, just enter the full path to Git Client and enter a description, as shown in the following screenshot:

If you set up only one Git installation and one Maven installation, Jenkins will always use these installations when needed. However, if for some you need to create multiple Git or Maven installations Jenkins, will provide a list box in the job configuration window to pick up the one to use. Click on the **Save** button to persist our changes, and let's now create the basic build job that will be triggered after every code check-in.

To do so, from the central Jenkins page, click on the **New item** link, located on the top-left of your screen, and you will be seeing something similar to the following image:

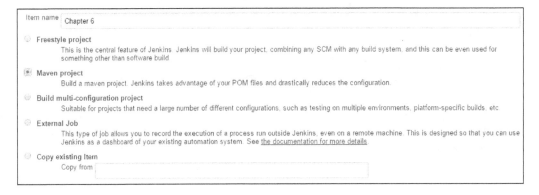

We are so in luck because Jenkins takes advantage of all the configurations we have been doing so far in the project's pom.xml file; so, we don't need to re-invent the wheel. Just enter an item's name, select **Maven project,** and click on the **OK** button.

In the project configuration page that follows, we will set up a few things regarding the project location and when build will run. First, locate the section labeled **Source Code Management**. If you have cloned our GitHub example, you can pick select Git or the corresponding one if you're using another SCM repository. Then, we need to specify the location of our root project. The following image illustrates the complete SCM configuration for the project of this book:

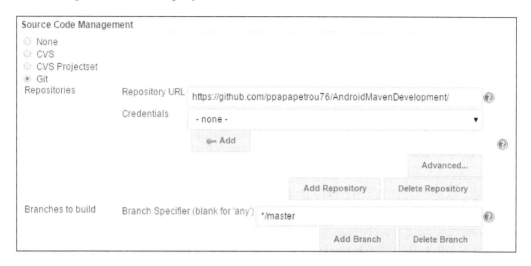

Now, it's time to tell Jenkins how to check for SCM changes and what to do when a change is found. Locate the **Build Triggers** section and select the **Build Periodically** option. In the text box that appears, enter the value of 0 0 0 0 0, five zeros separated by spaces in between, they would appear as * * * * * on the screen. This will tell Jenkins to check for changes every 1 minute. This is not the most efficient way, but for simplicity we decided to follow this path in our examples. Take a look at the following screenshot:

Finally, find the **Build** section and add the location of our root `pom.xml` file. Since we want to build only the example of this chapter, we add the value of `Chapter6/pom.xml` file in the **Root POM** field, and then we define the Maven goals. In our case, a simple "clean package" is enough for the post-commit build. Take a look at the following screenshot:

Save your changes and make some minor modifications in a project file. Check in the code and wait for Jenkins to join the game. If everything has been set up correctly, within the next minute you will see that a new build has been triggered and runs the goals we have defined in the previous section.

So far, we have done a small but crucial step toward automation. Every time a new code or a modified code is pushed to our GitHub repository, Jenkins will automatically build the project and run any unit tests, and so we will be aware of broken builds or failing tests as soon as the code is checked-in. And this is the essence of CI!

However, we haven't done anything about running integration tests and releasing/deploying our application. Similarly to what we have done for the post-commit build, we can create another job that will run only the integration tests. We have discussed in *Chapter 4, Integration Testing* how to create profiles and run with the proper Maven flags integration tests. You can just create a new Maven job and in the **Build** section enter the corresponding Maven goals. Usually, integration tests take more time than building and running unit tests; so, there are two recommended approaches for this:

- Run them only if the post-commit build is successful
- Run them only one time every night

There is no right or wrong on which is the best way to do it. Pick the one that suits better to your development style and your level of agility. A good point to start thinking is to measure how long do the integration tests take to finish. If you test your application across several devices and emulators and it takes some hours to execute all these tests, then this is a sign that running them in the nightly build is the best option.

The final step is to set up some jobs for releasing and optionally deploying your packages. Follow again the same steps to configure Jenkins, but this time make sure that the job is not triggered automatically. Usually, the official release should be done manually or automatically under certain circumstances (see for instance the promoted builds Jenkins plugin: `https://wiki.jenkins-ci.org/display/JENKINS/Promoted+Builds+Plugin`).

We highly recommend to set up a different job if you have multiple application modules in the same project, like we do in the example of this chapter (paid version versus free version). This way, you will be able to release and deploy only the desired version of your application. In the following matrix, we have summarized the strategy we have just discussed:

Build name	Automation level	Maven goals
Push commit build	Run after every check-in	Compile, run unit tests, generate debug-mode package
Integration tests	Run after every successful run of Post-Build Commit OR Run on a nightly basis	Compile and package with custom signing, obfuscator, and zipalign tasks. Run integration tests across many devices or emulators using the produced package
Release/Deploy	Manually on demand for each .apk of the project	Compile and package with custom signing, obfuscator, and zipalign tasks. Do a release and optionally deploy to a Maven repository

We have just scratched the surface of CI best practices and strategies when living in the Android world. This topic could easily fit in a complete book. Our focus was, however, to give you the basic knowledge and skills to implement a stable and well-defined automation strategy that will help you increase the productivity and streamline your development process. Based on our experience, not so many development teams follow these practices; so, we strongly encourage you to experiment with Jenkins or your favorite CI tool and try to automate as many possible activities for your project.

Summary

We are so excited that you have completed reading this important chapter. We know that Android developers struggle when it comes to proper package and release of an application to the public. We have analyzed in many details the necessary steps for a correct and complete packaging of Maven configuration. We also saw how to deploy the generated packages to a public or a local Maven repository and finally we discussed some automation best practices, and we went through some minimal examples on how to configure Jenkins to automatically run your builds, unit tests, integration tests, and release an application.

After finishing this chapter, you should have a solid knowledge of all the topics covered so far, and we expect that you have learned the following:

- When doing Android packaging is highly recommended to use a custom certificate, obfuscate, and zipalign the code
- Create your private certificate key
- Configure Maven for all the above steps using profiles
- Release an application
- Publish the generated packages to a Maven repository
- Understand the best CI and automation practices and be able to configure the required jobs in Jenkins CI tool

The last chapter can be considered as a bonus one. We will discuss tools and Maven plugins that will make the difference in any Android application development process.

7
Other Tools and Plugins

Welcome to the last chapter of this book. When we were figuring out the structure and contents of the chapters, there were some topics that we wanted to cover but didn't fit in any of the previous chapters. So, we decided to dedicate the last one to tools and Maven plugins that are worth your attention when you develop Android applications with Maven.

We had, however, two possible approaches. We had to list a big number of tools by just mentioning their basic characteristics or limit them to not more than a couple and discuss in detail how to effectively integrate them to your existing development process. The answer was easy, and we clearly prefer the latter. As this is a practical hands-on book, we want to provide you with as much as possible complete start-up guides for each of the tools presented in this chapter. After a lot of research, we end up to the following topics:

- Running static analysis using Android Lint
- Managing the quality of your code with SonarQube
- Boost the debugging and testing process with GenyMotion emulators

Both topics are presented through a step-by-step handbook, so you don't need to have any previous experience with the above-mentioned tools. All examples are based on the project we were looking at *Chapter 5, Android Flavors*, and *Chapter 6, Release Life Cycle and Continuous Integration*, and we are confident that by finishing this chapter you will be able to introduce and use them with your team.

Managing Android code quality

Over the last 2 or 3 years, there has been an increasing interest on managing software quality from a code perspective. Companies realize that having a healthy code base that allows development teams to quickly add new features, without creating regression bugs, is one of the basic keys to business success. Customers expect no less than a high-quality system. They demand quick adoption to rapid market changes without the fear of :*new version, new bugs, existing features broken*. This is why companies all over the globe are integrating numerous tools into their development process to manage and eventually improve the code quality of their large-scale systems. However, when it comes to mobile applications, people don't think the same way. For some, unexplainable reason, maybe it's the fact that the code base is not that large to manage quality. Or maybe the release cycles are too short to include that "strange quality thing." We believe the opposite. Mobile applications deserve to be managed from a quality perspective. The fact that some of them are downloaded and used by millions of users is enough to convince you. The larger is your target group, the more demands are created for your application. If you fail your customers once, you will not have a second chance. That's the ugly truth. On the other hand, setting up a complete quality tracking environment is not that hard as you think and this is what we will go through the next sections.

A short history about quality in Android

Although the first version of Android SDK was officially released back to 2008, the first Android specific quality tool (**Android Lint**) wasn't made available until 2011. Our experience has shown that not many Android applications are statistically analyzed with Lint.

According to Android's lint official web page:

> *The Android lint tool is a static code analysis tool that checks your Android project source files for potential bugs and optimization improvements for correctness, security, performance, usability, accessibility, and internationalization.*

Source:`http://developer.android.com/tools/help/lint.html`

When we were asking in the past people why they don't take advantage of Lint features the most popular answer that we got was "We cannot keep track if the quality is going up or down." For teams using Maven, things were even worse: "the Maven Android plugin doesn't support the execution of lint checks."

We are all in luck because things changed drastically. First of all, the android-maven-plugin, since version 3.5.1, officially supports the execution of Lint checks and can provide a well-structured report, so, yes, Maven houses can take advantage of Lint's static analysis. Later on, during the same year, **SonarQube** entered the game of Android quality management by releasing the first version of a plugin that leverages Android Lint's features in SonarQube ecosystem. This practically meant that SonarQube users could not only have their Android application analyzed by Lint but also get quality reports for all quality axis like complexity, duplications, test coverage, architecture, documentation, and so on.

SonarQube (http://www.sonarqube.org) is a free and open source system that very quickly has become the de facto standard for managing code quality. In a few words, it is a code-quality management platform that allows developer teams to manage, track, and eventually improve the quality of the source code. It's a web-based application that keeps historical data of a variety of metrics and gives trends of leading and lagging indicators for all seven deadly sins of developers.

The big difference/advantage of SonarQube is that you don't need to send quality reports to developers, but instead send the developers to view the reports in a nicely designed web dashboard with rich comparing and drill-down capabilities.

SonarQube supports more than 20 programming languages and it is integrated with the most popular quality tools like PMD, CheckStyle, FindBugs, and Lint.

Having said that, there is no excuse for treating source code quality of an Android application, as a second-class citizen. Everything is there, waiting for you, and you only need to do the right configuration. This is what we will discuss right away in the next sections.

Analyzing with Lint using Maven

Our first attempt to analyze our code will be by using the "lint" goal of the android-maven-plugin. By now, you should have seen several examples of enabling/disabling such goals, so it will be quite straightforward for you.

Edit the parent `pom.xml` file of our multimodule (free VS paid) application and make sure that the android-maven-plugin configuration looks like the following code snippet. The actual changes are displayed in code highlighted characters. Keep in mind also that these changes are done to the basic plugin configuration – not the release profile. We definitely want to have these checks running every time we build our code base:

```
<plugin>
    <groupId>com.jayway.maven.plugins.android.generation2</groupId>
    <artifactId>android-maven-plugin</artifactId>
    <extensions>true</extensions>
    <configuration>
        <sdk>
            <platform>19</platform>
        </sdk>
        <lint>
            <skip>false</skip>
            <enableHtml>true</enableHtml>
            <enableXml>false</enableXml>
        </lint>
    </configuration>
    <executions>
        <execution>
            <id>lint</id>
            <goals>
                <goal>lint</goal>
            </goals>
            <phase>install</phase>
        </execution>
    </executions>
</plugin>
```

Our changes target the plugin configuration and the goal execution. In short, we tell Maven to enable the execution of lint analysis and produce only an HTML report. Then, we instruct Maven to run the lint goal during the install phase. This is required because lint needs the `.apk` file which – like we saw in the previous chapter - is generated during the package phase. Now, we can simply run a clean build of our application including the "install" phase:

```
mvn clean install | grep -i Lint
```

For clarity, we have filtered out Maven output to produce only the logs related to lint execution. You should see something similar to the following screenshot:

```
[INFO] --- android-maven-plugin:3.8.2:lint (lint) @ FreeVersion ---
[INFO] Performing lint analysis.
[INFO] Writing Lint HTML report in C:\dev\android\packt\AndroidMavenDevelopment\Chapter7\F
reeVersion\target\lint-results\lint-results-html
[INFO] Running command: C:\dev\adt-bundle-windows-x86_64-20131030\sdk\tools\lint.bat
[INFO] with parameters: [--showall, --html, C:\dev\android\packt\AndroidMavenDevelopment\C
hapter7\FreeVersion\target\lint-results\lint-results-html, --sources, C:\dev\android\packt
\AndroidMavenDevelopment\Chapter7\FreeVersion\src\main\java, C:\dev\android\packt\AndroidM
avenDevelopment\Chapter7\FreeVersion, --exitcode]
[INFO] Lint analysis completed successfully.
[INFO] --- android-maven-plugin:3.8.2:lint (lint) @ PaidVersion ---
[INFO] Performing lint analysis.
[INFO] Writing Lint HTML report in C:\dev\android\packt\AndroidMavenDevelopment\Chapter7\P
aidVersion\target\lint-results\lint-results-html
[INFO] Running command: C:\dev\adt-bundle-windows-x86_64-20131030\sdk\tools\lint.bat
[INFO] with parameters: [--showall, --html, C:\dev\android\packt\AndroidMavenDevelopment\C
hapter7\PaidVersion\target\lint-results\lint-results-html, --sources, C:\dev\android\packt
\AndroidMavenDevelopment\Chapter7\PaidVersion\src\main\java, C:\dev\android\packt\AndroidM
avenDevelopment\Chapter7\PaidVersion, --exitcode]
[INFO] Lint analysis completed successfully.
```

Now, you can browse the generated report, which can be found under `target/lint-results/lint-results-html` directory of each module. For instance, the following image illustrates the report you can see if you open the `index.html` file of the `CommonLibrary` module:

You can explore the rest of the report by yourself. Just click on the module link and you will see a list of the reported issues with detailed explanation, compliant and non-compliant code, and a classification of severity. You will also see a list of all disabled rules. Explaining all the rules of Android Lint is out of the scope of this book, so we highly recommend you to explore the complete rule-set and understand the purpose and impact of each rule.

Unleashing the power of SonarQube

We made a small step toward managing quality. By now, you are able to manually analyze the application code using Maven. However, we lack automation. One way to do this is to modify the `postcommit` Jenkins job we discussed in *Chapter 6, Release Life Cycle and Continuous Integration*, and include the install phase in our Maven execution goals. This way, every time someone checks in code in the SCM repository, a new Lint analysis will be available as an HTML report.

This status has two drawbacks. First, there's no way to automatically figure out if the latest check-in introduced new issues or if any of the previous detected issues have been resolved. In other words, we cannot compare two quality snapshots. Furthermore, identifying rule violations is only a small part of the code quality. We have no reporting about complexity or duplications.

SonarQube comes to the rescue and can offer us everything that lint does, plus a lot of meaningful metric. In this section, we will explain how to configure SonarQube and run a complete analysis of our example application. Downloading and installing SonarQube is easy by following the instructions that can be found at `http://www.sonarqube.org/downloads/` and `http://docs.sonarqube.org/display/SONAR/Setup+and+Upgrade`.

For simplicity, you can keep the default settings without setting up a database. We also recommend that you install the latest **Long-Term Supported (LTS)** version. At the time of writing this book, the latest LTS was 4.5.1.

The SonarQube after it's installed looks something like the following:

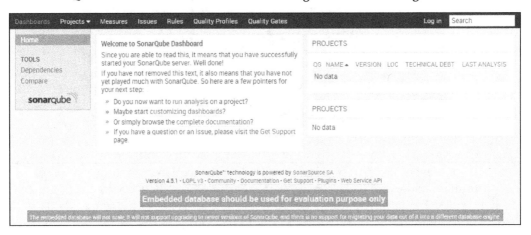

After completing the installation, you can access the web dashboard by typing this URL in your web browser: `http://localhost:9000` and you should see the main page as shown in the preceding image. Don't worry about the big red letters warning you that you are using the embedded database. This is absolutely fine for our demonstration purposes.

The default installation of SonarQube doesn't ship with the Android rules, so we need to manually install the corresponding plugin. First, you need to log in as an administrator (`username/password : admin/admin`). Once logged in, click on the **Settings** link, which is on the top right of your screen and then on the **Update Center** option on the left menu, under the **SYSTEM** section, and this is shown in the following screenshot:

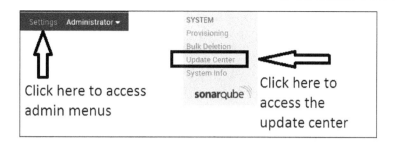

Finally, click on the **Available plugins** tab, move down to the **LANGUAGES** section, and click on the Android plugin. After installing it, you need to restart SonarQube to complete installation and prepare the plugin for utilization. To verify that everything was done properly, you can go back to the update center and check that the Android plugin appears under the **Installed plugins** tab.

Now that our SonarQube installation is ready, let's configure Maven and then analyze our sample project. We want to create a global SonarQube profile, so edit the `%M2_HOME%/conf/settings.xml` file and add the following code snippet under the `<profiles>` element:

```
<profile>
  <id>sonar</id>
    <activation>
      <activeByDefault>true</activeByDefault>
    </activation>
  <properties>
    <sonar.jdbc.url>
      jdbc:h2:tcp://localhost:9092/sonar
    </sonar.jdbc.url>
    <sonar.jdbc.username>sonar</sonar.jdbc.username>
    <sonar.jdbc.password>sonar</sonar.jdbc.password>
  </properties>
</profile>
```

The above configuration is valid only for the embedded database. If you want to use SonarQube for a production environment, it is strongly advised that you set up to use a real database. In that case, you need to modify the `<sonar.jdbc.url>` to the corresponding JDBC URL. For instance, if you plan to use MySQL then the JDBC URL will probably look like this:

```
jdbc:mysql://localhost:3306/sonar?useUnicode=true
&amp;characterEncoding=utf8
```

It is time to run our first SonarQube analysis. Just open a terminal window, navigate to the folder where the parent `pom.xml` file is located, and type the following Maven commands:

```
mvn clean install
mvn sonar:sonar -Dsonar.profile="Android Lint" | grep -i Sonar
```

The first command will run a typical clean build of our application. The second will trigger a SonarQube analysis with the Quality profile named `Android Lint`. The command will also filter out only the Maven output which is related to SonarQube to make it easier to check that the analysis has been completed successfully.

Accessing SonarQube's UI again, we will find a new entry (**Chapter 7-Quality**, that is the name of our sample project) under the PROJECTS section. Verify that your screen is looking like the following image:

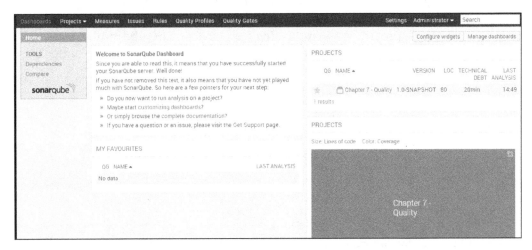

The name of the projects is a clickable link that will redirect us to the project's dashboard. See the following image. A lot of things and numbers are shown on that page. In short, the dashboard is composed of widgets that report on a different quality axis. For example, you can see the information about the complexity, the duplicated lines of code, the number of issues reported (yes, that's Android Lint), and the technical debt ratio and other statistics about the size of the project. If you make some changes on the code and run a new analysis again, on the top of your screen you can see a drop-down list box with the text "Time changes". Picking a delta (δ) period, for instance "since previous analysis", the dashboard will slightly change and will provide some additional reporting. You will see a comparison between the previous analysis and the current analysis. This will make it easy to understand if your project is doing well or the quality is going up or down.

Looks awesome, right? But something is missing from this dashboard. Can you figure out what? What's one of the important quality axis that is not displayed in the page we are looking at? Correct. Code coverage. We have spent two chapters in this book to discuss about testing our application in all layers and SonarQube doesn't support it? Don't worry, reporting on test coverage is one of the most important things reported by SonarQube, but SonarQube itself doesn't run tests. We need to tell it where to find the unit test results and the code coverage report, and this is shown in the following image:

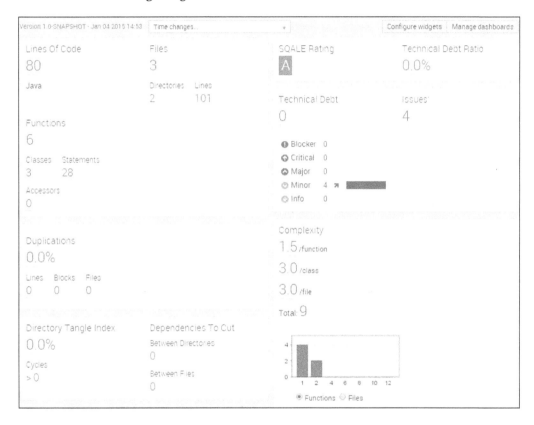

So far, we haven't configured **JaCoCo** for the Paid VS Free Maven project, but we to leave that to you as an exercise. You can follow the steps we explained in *Chapter 3, Unit Testing*, and prepare the corresponding Maven profile.

Implement the profile on the parent project to make it available to all submodules. You can also use **Robolectric** in the project to add a very simple Unit test and see how the coverage is reported on SonarQube. Both can be found on the GitHub repository where the code of this book is located.

We will focus on configuring SonarQube through Maven to read the test coverage reports and produce some nice UI widgets on the project dashboard. Add the following properties in the parent `pom.xml` file:

```
<sonar.junit.reportsPath>target/surefire-reports</sonar.junit.
reportsPath>
<sonar.java.coveragePlugin>jacoco</sonar.java.coveragePlugin>
<sonar.jacoco.reportPath>target/jacoco.exec</sonar.jacoco.reportPath>
<sonar.profile>Android Lint</sonar.profile>
```

The following properties will instruct SonarQube to reuse the existing reports generated by our favorite tools – Surefire and JaCoCo Maven plugins in our case. The first property (`sonar.junit.reportsPath`) tells SonarQube where to find the unit tests execution reports generated by surefire. Next, we tell SonarQube that our code coverage tool is "jacoco" (`sonar.java.coveragePlugin`). Finally, we let SonarQube know where to find the code coverage report (`sonar.jacoco.reportPath`). As a bonus property, we added the `sonar.profile` property we previously used to simplify our command line execution.

> If you want to experiment a little more, you can also create a cobertura profile and set the value of the `sonar.java.coveragePlugin` property to cobertura. In that case, you need to set `sonar.cobertura.reportPath` property instead to a value that points to cobertura file (that is: `target/cobertura/cobertura.ser`).

We can now run again a SonarQube analysis by executing the following Maven commands on the directory where the parent `pom.xml` file is located:

```
mvn clean install -Pjacoco
mvn sonar:sonar
```

Going back to the project's dashboard, we will be able to see another widget that will report on test execution and test coverage. It will look like the following image, although the numbers may vary depending on how many tests you have written and how many lines are hit by these tests. In our case, the numbers tell us that we have implemented two test cases that cover almost half of our code base:

Unit Tests Coverage	Unit Test Success
48.5%	100.0%
Line Coverage	Failures Errors Tests
48.5%	0 0 2
	Execution Time
	7.3 sec

Now, everything is set and you can continue playing around with SonarQube. You can click on any number you see on the widgets and drill down to module, package, or file level. This way, you will find out the exact location of an issue, a duplication block of lines, a not covered by tests method, or even a complex piece of code.

SonarQube is a great product and clearly we cannot cover all its star features in a few pages. There are several resources on the Internet including the official documentation page (`http://docs.sonarqube.org/`) where you can read and find out all the ways you can use it to continuously inspect the quality of an Android application. You can also find articles and guidelines that will help you to integrate it with other powerful and popular tools, like Jenkins, and make it a part of your development process. We hope that the quick overview we did is fair enough to excite your curiosity and explore it more.

Boost development speed with GenyMotion

Every developer who writes Android application has used the emulators provided by Android SDK to test and/or debug the code under development. I bet that there's no one out there who hasn't been frustrated about the time the emulator needs to load, deploy the application, and run it. Things are getting even worse when you want to test large applications with time-consuming activities, in a limited-resources environment.

The answer to these problems is called **GenyMotion** (`https://www.genymotion.com/`) and it comes in two flavors: free and commercial. We will focus on the free features that are enough to leave behind forever the old-fashioned Android SDK emulators. So what is actually GenyMotion? Why is it so fast and what are the advantages of using it over Android emulators?

GenyMotion is actually an Android running on **VirtualBox** (`https://www.virtualbox.org/`) virtual machine (VM). VirtualBox is a visualization platform for home and enterprise usages that can be run on almost every available operating system of the market. It is so fast that some times Android applications start up even faster than real devices. The key benefits of using GenyMotion includes but not limited to are as follows:

- Supports all known operating systems like Windows, Linux, and Mac.
- It is integrated with the most popular Android development tools like Eclipse and Android Studio.

- Supports a variety of sensors like battery, temperature, GPS, and many more. Thus, developers can run tests and simulate real-world scenarios by just using the emulator.

- Has **x86** supports and ships with numerous preconfigured VMs. This practically means that you don't need to spend even a minute to configure these VMs.

- Supports device rotation, WiFi simulation, and can use the web camera of the hosting environment to test camera-related features.

- Supports the most popular Android APIs starting from version 10 (2.3.7) up to the latest version 21 (5.0)

There is only one problem with GenyMotion. Like we said, sometimes it runs even faster than real devices, so we recommend that you test your applications to a real device as well to make sure that they have the expected behavior. Actually, even if you don't use GenyMotion it is not good practice to manually or automatically test your applications only in emulators. Many things look and more importantly behave differently when you run your code on a real device.

Deploying our example to a GenyMotion emulator

You can download and install the free version of GenyMotion by following the instructions found on the official website: `http://www.genymotion.com`. You should create an account and download the binary for your operating system. The instructions are very well documented, so you won't have any difficulties. If you don't have VirtualBox installed, you will need to install it as well but don't worry. You will find two available downloads for each GenyMotion version on their site. One binary including VirtualBox and one without it. We strongly also recommend to install the plugin for your favorite Integrated Development Enviroment (IDE) (**Eclipse** or Android Studio).

During the next sections, we will guide you to create an emulator based on the project configuration settings and deploy our sample application. When we are done with installing GenyMotion, we can start the management console. There is also a command line interface but command-line lovers but for clarity we will stick on to the graphical interface. This has been depicted in the following screenshot:

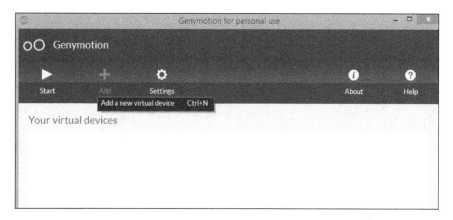

Let's begin now:

1. Our first step is to create a new emulator VM. Remember from our project configuration that our target SDK platform is version 19, so we should create an emulator built on that version:

    ```
    <sdk>
      <platform>19</platform>
    </sdk>
    ```

2. Click on the **Add** button of the GenyMotion VM management console. It will pop up a dialog box with all the available preconfigured virtual devices.

3. On the top left of that dialog, select the desired Android version, that is, 4.4.4 (SDK 19) in our case.

4. Scroll down to the filtered list and locate the device named: Samsung Galaxy Note 3 - 4.4.4 - API 19 - 1080x1920.

5. Click on next, and enter a different name if you want. At the same page, you can review the default configuration of that device. Isn't it so cool that you don't need to care about the number of megabytes that are needed to run this device or how many disk space is suggested to be reserved? We love flexibility but in this case we tend to prefer stability over flexibility. This has been depicted in the following screenshot:

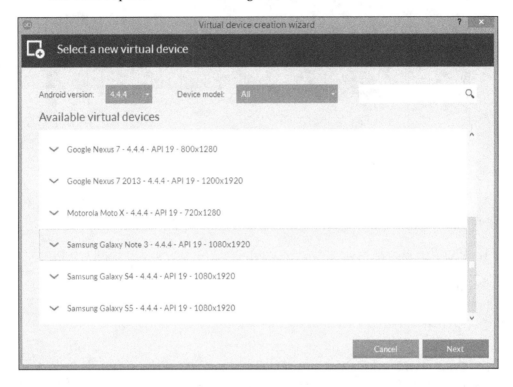

The Android instance is probably not downloaded, so GenyMotion will do that for you. This will take some minutes depending on your Internet connection. Typically, each VM is about 200 MB. When the download is complete, the image will be displayed in the list of available emulators. You can select it and click on the **Start** button. In less than a few seconds, your emulator is up and running and waiting for you to use it.

Let us try to deploy our sample application with the typical way we have discussed in *Chapter 2, Starting the Development Phase*. Keep the emulator running and open again a terminal window. Navigate to the "Free version" directory end type the following command:

```
mvn android:deploy | grep -i GenyMotion
```

The deployment should not take more than 1 – 2 seconds. If you try to compare this number with the time needed to deploy to a real device, you will probably notice that it takes almost half time. The (filtered with the term `GenyMotion`) Maven output will probably look like the following image:

```
[INFO] Device 192.168.56.100_5555_Genymotion_SamsungGalaxyNote3-4.4.4-API19-1080x1920 foun
d.
[INFO] 192.168.56.100_5555_Genymotion_SamsungGalaxyNote3-4.4.4-API19-1080x1920 :    Success
fully uninstalled com.packt.androidmaven.free from 192.168.56.100_5555_Genymotion_SamsungG
alaxyNote3-4.4.4-API19-1080x1920
[INFO] Device 192.168.56.100_5555_Genymotion_SamsungGalaxyNote3-4.4.4-API19-1080x1920 foun
d.
[INFO] 192.168.56.100_5555_Genymotion_SamsungGalaxyNote3-4.4.4-API19-1080x1920 :    Success
fully installed C:\dev\android\packt\AndroidMavenDevelopment\Chapter7\FreeVersion\target\F
reeVersion.apk to 192.168.56.100_5555_Genymotion_SamsungGalaxyNote3-4.4.4-API19-1080x1920
```

You can now use the GenyMotion emulator and manually test our application. It will run super-fast! A very interesting exercise for you would be to add some instrumentation tests using **Robotium** or **Selendroid**. Both tools were covered in *Chapter 4, Integration Testing*. Then, create the proper Maven configuration and run the tests against our GenyMotion emulator. Keep track of the time needed to run all tests and then do the same but now using a standard Android emulator. Then, you can run them once again but this time use a real device. It will be really amazing to see and compare the results of each test execution.

GenyMotion, however, is not just another, faster and easier to use Android emulator. It can be used also as an extension to your favorite testing framework and write tests for a variety of sensors such as battery, camera, GPS, WiFi, multitouch, and others. And the best of it is that you can integrate it with Maven by adding a single dependency.

Unfortunately the best things in life don't come for free and all these fancy features are only available in the commercial edition, so we cannot discuss them in detail, as they are not part of the free version of GenyMotion. We strongly recommend you, especially if you are writing Android applications for a software house and you want to speed up your development and testing process to give this tool a try. We believe it to be worth the effort.

Summary

This is the end! You have now mastered *Android application development with Maven* and you are confident that Maven has nothing to be jealous from Ant or even Gradle. We have discussed many times throughout this book of how every software development activity can be simplified using declarative configuration and make it part of the project itself with no advanced scripting knowledge or hard to understand settings. The power of Maven – plugins – hides all the technical details and lets you describe what you want to do in each phase. The rest is Maven's job, and by now you should be convinced that it really does a pretty good job on that.

Our last chapter was dedicated to two different topics. We first covered the critical but overlooked practice of managing code quality. We explored ways of analyzing an application's source code. At the beginning, we saw how to configure Android Lint and then we explained the advantages of SonarQube over a typical static-code analyzer. We also ran a full analysis of our sample project and we saw what kind of quality numbers we get by SonarQube. The last part of this book was dedicated to an alternative toolset of emulators: GenyMotion. Although it is not related directly to Maven, it works very well with what we have discussed in the previous chapter and boosts the development and debugging speed.

After finishing the last chapter of this book, we expect that you have gained a solid knowledge of SonarQube and GenyMotion and you are able to:

- Configure and run Android Lint analysis using Maven
- Configure and run SonarQube analysis using Maven
- Understand the advantages of SonarQube over a static-code analyzer
- Use GenyMotion emulators instead of the standard emulators provided by Android SDK

So, this is the end of the book. We really hope you enjoyed the journey and you found a lot of useful practical tips. Feel free to tweet about this book, write a blog review, or just drop us an e-mail with your feedback. Good luck on your next Android – *Mavenized-* project!

Index

stopping by default, with mvn
     android:emulator-stop command 44
stopping, mvn android:emulator-stop
     command used 44
undeploying, with mvn android:undeploy
     command 46, 47

B

Bamboo
  URL 150
Bitnami
  URL 151
build profiles
  creating 108
  separation, by library 117-128
  separation, by packaging 109-117

C

Cobertura
  about 80
  using 80
Continuous Integration (CI)
  about 131, 150
  best practices 150-155

D

Dalvik 42
Data Access Object (DAO) 48
Distribution Management 147

E

Eclipse
  about 15, 168
  Android SDK integration 15-18
  Maven integration 15-18
  project, creating 18-20
  project, importing 30
  setting up 15-18
Espresso
  about 103
  URL 103

G

General Public License (GPL) 49
GenyMotion
  about 167
  benefits 167
  example, deploying to 168-171
  URL 167, 168
  used, for boosting development speed 167
global level, Maven profiles 108
Graphical User Interface (GUI)
  about 37
  used, for creating AVD 37, 38

H

HotSpot 42

I

IDE
  about 7
  Eclipse 15
  IntelliJ IDEA 21
  Maven, integration 15
  NetBeans 28
in-command line
  used, for creating AVD 38-40
installation
  Android SDK 9-12
  Java Runtime Environment (JRE) 7
  JDK7 7
instrumentation testing
  about 83
  fundamentals 84
Integrated Development Environment. *See*
     IDE
integration testing
  about 59
  Graphical User Interface (GUI) testing 83
  instrumentation testing 83
IntelliJ IDEA
  about 9, 21
  Android SDK integration 21
  Maven integration 21

Maven integration, specific to Android
  Studio 22
plugins, enabling 24
project importing, specific to Android
  Studio 25-28
setting up 21
URL, for downloading 21

J

Java Code Coverage (JaCoCo)
  about 77, 165
  URL 77
  using 77-79
Java Development Kit (JDK) 7
Java Runtime Environment (JRE)
  installing 7, 8
  URL 7
Java Virtual Machine (JVM) 72
JDK7
  installing 7, 8
  URL, for downloading 7
Jenkins
  URL 150
Jetty 55
JRockit 42

L

Lollipop 11

M

Maven
  downloading 8
  integration, with IDE 15
  project, creating 12-14
  URL, for downloading 8
Maven Central Repository 13
Maven profiles
  about 107
  global level 108
  project level 108
  user level 108
Model-View-Controller (MVC) 54
mvn android:deploy command
  used, for deploying AVD 45, 46

mvn android:emulator-start command
  used, for starting AVD 43, 44
mvn android:emulator-stop command
  used, for stopping all AVD 44
  used, for stopping AVD by default 44
mvn android:undeploy command
  used, for undeploying AVD 46, 47

N

NetBeans
  about 28
  Android SDK integration 28-30
  Maven integration 28-30
  setting up 28, 29
  URL, for downloading 28

O

obfuscation 138

P

ProGuard
  about 138
  URL 140
project level, Maven profiles 108
Project Object Model (POM) 14
ProviderTestCase2 class 84

R

release process, Android application
  about 144
  local repository, deploying 147-150
  performing, without deployment to
    repository 144-146
Robolectric
  about 165
  configuring, with maven 73
  unit testing 72
  unit tests, running 73-76
Robotium
  about 95, 171
  URL 95
  working with 95-98

S

Selendroid
about 98, 171
configuring 98-101
UI tests, writing for Maven native
applications 101, 102
URL 98
used, for UI tests 98
Selenium 98
ServiceTestCase class 84
Software Development Kit (SDK) 34
SonarQube
about 159
advantage 159
download link 162
features 162
URL 159
used, for managing code quality 162-167
Source Control Management (SCM)
tool 134
Spoon
about 89
configuring, with Maven 90-94
reports, viewing 94, 95
running 94, 95
screenshots, grabbing with 89, 90
URL 90

T

TeamCity
URL 150
test coverage
Cobertura 80
JaCoCo 77
measuring 76

testing

integration testing 59
unit testing 59
Tomcat 55
tools, integration testing
about 103
Appium 104
Espresso 103
Travis
URL 150

U

UI tests
with Selendroid 98
unit testing
about 59
Android applications, testing 59, 60
running 60-64
test coverage, measuring 76
with Robolectric 72
user level, Maven profiles 108

V

VirtualBox
about 167
URL 167

Z

zipalign 141

Thank you for buying
Android Application Development with Maven

About Packt Publishing

Packt, pronounced 'packed', published its first book, *Mastering phpMyAdmin for Effective MySQL Management*, in April 2004, and subsequently continued to specialize in publishing highly focused books on specific technologies and solutions.

Our books and publications share the experiences of your fellow IT professionals in adapting and customizing today's systems, applications, and frameworks. Our solution-based books give you the knowledge and power to customize the software and technologies you're using to get the job done. Packt books are more specific and less general than the IT books you have seen in the past. Our unique business model allows us to bring you more focused information, giving you more of what you need to know, and less of what you don't.

Packt is a modern yet unique publishing company that focuses on producing quality, cutting-edge books for communities of developers, administrators, and newbies alike. For more information, please visit our website at www.packtpub.com.

About Packt Open Source

In 2010, Packt launched two new brands, Packt Open Source and Packt Enterprise, in order to continue its focus on specialization. This book is part of the Packt Open Source brand, home to books published on software built around open source licenses, and offering information to anybody from advanced developers to budding web designers. The Open Source brand also runs Packt's Open Source Royalty Scheme, by which Packt gives a royalty to each open source project about whose software a book is sold.

Writing for Packt

We welcome all inquiries from people who are interested in authoring. Book proposals should be sent to author@packtpub.com. If your book idea is still at an early stage and you would like to discuss it first before writing a formal book proposal, then please contact us; one of our commissioning editors will get in touch with you.

We're not just looking for published authors; if you have strong technical skills but no writing experience, our experienced editors can help you develop a writing career, or simply get some additional reward for your expertise.

Learning Apache Maven 3 [Video]

ISBN: 978-1-78216-666-5   Duration: 01:59 hours

Get to grips with the basics and concepts of building a real-world Java application with Apache Maven

1. A practical example-driven approach to learning Apache Maven 3.

2. Grasp the fundamentals and extend Apache Maven 3 to meet your needs.

3. Learn to use Apache Maven with Java, Enterprise Frameworks, and various other cutting-edge technologies.

Maven Build Customization

ISBN: 978-1-78398-722-1   Paperback: 270 pages

Discover the real power of Maven 3 to manage your Java projects more effectively than ever

1. Administer complex projects customizing the Maven framework and improving the software lifecycle of your organization with "Maven friend technologies".

2. Automate your delivery process and make it fast and easy.

3. An easy-to-follow tutorial on Maven customization and integration with a real project and practical examples.

Please check **www.PacktPub.com** for information on our titles

Instant Apache Maven Starter

ISBN: 978-1-78216-760-0   Paperback: 62 pages

Get started with the fundamentals of developing Java projects with Apache Maven

1. Learn something new in an Instant! A short, fast, focused guide delivering immediate results.

2. Create Java projects and project templates with Maven archetypes.

3. Manage project dependencies, project coordinates, and multi-modules.

4. Download, install, and configure Maven on different operating systems.

Android User Interface Development Beginner's Guide

ISBN: 978-1-84951-448-4   Paperback: 304 pages

Quickly design and develop compelling user interfaces for your Android applications

1. Leverage the Android platform's flexibility and power to design impactful user-interfaces.

2. Build compelling, user-friendly applications that will look great on any Android device.

3. Make your application stand out from the rest with styles and themes.

4. A practical beginner's guide to take you step-by-step through the process of developing user interfaces to get your applications noticed!

Please check **www.PacktPub.com** for information on our titles

www.ingramcontent.com/pod-product-compliance
Lightning Source LLC
LaVergne TN
LVHW081342050326
832903LV00024B/1267